T0306991

What People Are Say

Be Like the Wind

A dear friend, a nun, referred me to Ellen 13 years ago. An experienced cat rescuer, I was stuck. One of my sweetest kitties had become aggressive to a new rescue. The problem was simple if one can talk to cats, thus Ellen resolved that problem overnight. Ellen is authentic. She became an indispensable part of caring for my rescues. Her energy work kept my cat in chemotherapy, eating. I would never have found a missing cat without her guidance. Litterbox aggression by another new rescue? Past life intrusion. Solution? Custom flower essences that she dowsed with a pendulum for the aggressor. Ellen's compassion, intuition, skill, insight, and ability to communicate with animals (present and no longer with us) led me to extoll her gifts. She has aided dozens of friends and friends of friends. I cannot think of a better person for whom to provide a platform. Ellen does not just have a gift. Ellen is the gift.
Laurie Goldstein, Food Fur Life

I have known Ellen Kohn for 20 years. She is a magnificent psychic and my go-to healer when I need insight into anything I cannot see for myself. Ellen is an expert animal communicator and a loving beautiful oracle doing sacred work with animals and humans every day. I have been aware of her diligent work on this manuscript over the last several years. The messages she received from the horses are full of vital and timeless wisdom that needs to be spread into the world in these troubled times for the benefit of all beings on the planet. Ellen is insightful, thoughtful, and thorough, as well as incredibly intuitive and spiritual.
Reverend Heidi Saltzman, shaman, spiritual counselor, psychic and psychologist

Ellen Kohn is a gifted animal communicator, healer and spiritual counsellor who was a regular writer for *Dogs Naturally Magazine* during our ten years of publishing a print magazine, from 2011 to 2021. She contributed articles to our bimonthly publication several times a year. Ellen's articles were always extremely well-written, with strong attention to detail, and required almost no editing. She approached unusual, often spiritual topics in a sensitive and practical way that made them clear and accessible to readers with little knowledge of the subject matter. She was one of our more popular contributors.

Ellen also helped many readers with their own animals. She's helped me immensely with my own dogs. Ellen's loving ability to connect with an animal is extraordinary, especially at stressful times like end-of-life. She brings comfort and closure to hospice-stage care and decision-making for a beloved pet. The animals feel heard as well, which helps ease their transition and is a blessing to all.

Julia Henriques, Managing Editor, *Dogs Naturally Magazine*

To know Ellen Kohn is to be blessed on a deep profound spiritual level. Ellen has been part of my life for over ten years. Ellen is a gifted medium and empath equally at home with people and her beloved animals. She's done psychic as well as mediumistic readings for so many with extreme accuracy. She has participated in many classes at the Santa Fe Institute for Mediumship and Spiritual Studies. She is especially gifted with her beloved horses, who have always been an important part of her life.

Once when visiting Ellen, she was remotely searching for a lost Canadian dog. She asked the owners to go back where they already looked. They were reluctant, but sure enough, their dog was precisely where Ellen said it would be. Speaking of dogs, she did a reading on my dog, Gus, revealing amazing information, including past life connections. Ellen's strong

connection to Spirit has repeatedly been proven. For that reason, we anxiously await her new book about her kinship to her horses. I'm sure it will reveal profound information long overdue.
Kevin Bruce Horton, Santa Fe Institute for Mediumship and Spiritual Studies

A beautiful and unique spiritual book with channeled information directly from horses to humans. An absolute MUST-READ!
G.L. Davies, author *Harvest: The True Story of Alien Abduction*

Be Like the Wind

Three Equines Channel Spiritual Light

Be Like the Wind

Three Equines Channel Spiritual Light

Ellen Kohn

6TH
BOOKS

London, UK
Washington, DC, USA

CollectiveInk

First published by Sixth Books, 2024
Sixth Books is an imprint of Collective Ink Ltd.,
Unit 11, Shepperton House, 89 Shepperton Road, London, N1 3DF
office@collectiveinkbooks.com
www.collectiveinkbooks.com
www.6th-books.com

For distributor details and how to order please visit the 'Ordering' section on our website.

Text copyright: Ellen Kohn 2023

ISBN: 978 1 80341 601 4
978 1 80341 619 9 (ebook)
Library of Congress Control Number: 2023941657

All rights reserved. Except for brief quotations in critical articles or reviews, no part of this book may be reproduced in any manner without prior written permission from the publishers.

The rights of Ellen Kohn as author have been asserted in accordance with the Copyright, Designs and Patents Act 1988.

A CIP catalogue record for this book is available from the British Library.

Design: Lapiz Digital Services

UK: Printed and bound by CPI Group (UK) Ltd, Croydon, CR0 4YY
Printed in North America by CPI GPS partners

We operate a distinctive and ethical publishing philosophy in all areas of our business, from our global network of authors to production and worldwide distribution.

Contents

Be Like the Wind is dedicated to our son, Phil Kohn,
who died on May 5, 2023.
Godspeed our Beloved.

Foreword

Dear reader, you now hold a very special book written by a remarkable woman. Ellen Kohn is one of the kindest, most gentle, and perceptive people on the planet. She is a sensitive, an empath, a mediumistic healer, and I am lucky to call her my friend and colleague. This book is what many call a "channeled book," meaning her horses communicated with Ellen telepathically so she could tell their stories to you. Some people may rather see these stories as "inspired by Ellen's relationship with her horses," and others may better understand these stories as seen through the eyes of horses.

Ellen has a long history as an animal communicator, healer, psychic/medium, and philanthropist. One of the first times I met Ellen, she was helping a family in another country find their lost dog using her psychic and mediumistic abilities. I later learned she successfully finds such animals on a regular basis.

Working with Ellen in any capacity is inspiring. You will undoubtedly deepen your relationship with yourself, other people, and animals after reading *Be Like the Wind*. If you are a sensitive, you will easily understand the energies poured out on these pages. Horse people will relate to it and gain insights. If you're not one of the above, I challenge you to either read it as a touching work of nonfiction seen from a psychic angle, or just perhaps, approach it as a work of magical realism. Whatever your approach, if you enjoy this book as I did, you too will *Be Like the Wind*.

Gerald R. Schoelzel, Esq.

Medium and Lover of Animals

Acknowledgements

A heartfelt thank you to Billy, Monty and Romeo for inviting me to channel their life stories into *Be Like the Wind*. They transformed their thoughts, feelings and emotions into messages that convey the importance of Spirit in our lives.

I am grateful for Heidi Saltzman's intuitive creations that birthed *Be Like the Wind*'s illustrations.

Mental and emotional support was provided by my family, and my spiritual community. My husband, Steve, was the best sounding board any budding author could have. Special thanks to Gerald Schoelzel, Kevin Horton, and Heidi Saltzman for their faith in me to wordsmith the horses' communiques.

Technical help was critical to *Be Like the Wind*'s publication. For that, I thank my son, Rob Kohn, and my friend, Olivier Renard.

I am blessed to know Spirit's magic. Divine intelligence provides a stalwart ally, helping me navigate the inevitable challenges that surface in my life. With my angels and Spirit guides by my side, I have an unshakable nexus to the universe.

Introduction

Who knew the equine world would nominate three horses to write a book about spirituality? One human horse whisperer would relay their communiques through their stories and life lessons. In a compassionate and warmhearted style, the horses submit their advice for the betterment of humanity.

Preface

The Genesis

The genesis for *Be Like the Wind* began on horseback. A dynamic energy flooded the atmosphere, charging it with inquisitiveness and excitement. I could feel something big was about to happen as Monty and I left the barn to savor our alone time together.

It was an exhilarating feeling.

Monty was a calm and amenable partner, enriching our rides with his gentle and soft personality. We had no agenda except to enjoy each other's company while taking in the breathtaking scenery around us. My main riding buddy, he took the lead while we meandered along our favorite trails.

Most days I rode alone, listening to spiritual tunes on my phone. Attached to my saddle pack, the music came through clearly. Setting a relaxing atmosphere for both of us, the melodies invited access to the Spirit realm around us.

The serene and peaceful terrain was conducive to stillness, creating the perfect backdrop for interspecies communication to manifest. And it did.

This day was different. Energy built between me and Monty, creating a palpable connection. Spirit was calling me to create a record of the extraordinary communication growing between us. Out of the blue, a question popped out of my mouth, asking him for his life advice.

Monty immediately replied, "Be like the wind." Stunned, I knew I was supposed to write down his words in my phone, recording verbatim what his message implied. In one timely moment, the script for *Be Like the Wind* was disclosed.

Being one of the most psychic horses I'd ever known, Monty was the first of many to speak his truth, revealing the purpose of this book. His gentle yet powerful messages inspired me to dig deeper, seeking the unspoken words from many of the horses I had shared my life with. As it turns out, a master plan had been co-created by three horses over the course of many years and countless adventures.

> *The seeds for Be Like the Wind were planted long before I met Monty.*

In hindsight, the actual unfolding of the process began in 1990 when I met the wonderful thoroughbred, Billy Bend. He was the horse who changed my world. Like Monty, Billy was chosen by the Equine Council to initiate a psychic connection with me. His outgoing personality, confidence, and curiosity about horse-human relationships made him the perfect candidate to consecrate the initial Spirit-to-Spirit communications.

> *Entering a place of pure serenity when we were together was effortless.*

While Romeo is the third horse to join the other two collaborators, he brings his own distinct style to these chapters. His subtle, big-hearted energy prompts me to "lead with love" in this chaotic world, an aspiring quality we all can emulate.

Each horse brought a new perspective on the Divine connection, expanding the book's material while strengthening the metaphysical intelligence. As the puzzle pieces began to fit together, *Be Like the Wind* was birthed.

When I realized this special group of equines had communed spiritually to guide the book's publication, it was an amazing awakening to the power of the unified field of consciousness.

Thanks to the lessons Billy, Monty and Romeo taught me, my life has undergone a complete metamorphosis. Infused into my entire being, their spiritual impact is ongoing. At the time of this writing Romeo and I continue to explore our spiritual journey together.

And so, the magic lives on.

Part I

Spirit Materializes

Chapter 1

Spirit Appeals

Through the Horses' Lens

We introduce ourselves with our nicknames: Billy, Monty and Romeo. We are responding to a spiritual appeal, a call to action. Our collective effort has resulted in *Be Like the Wind*'s written material. These are our personal stories and teachings that infuse its pages. From this point forward, we speak in first person, addressing you directly. The chapters are presented from our perspective, and we speak for all animals, everywhere on Earth.

Spirit has demonstrated horse energy signifies one of the most powerful forces on the planet. In preparation for global transformation and healing, horse was chosen to mentor and guide humans through a period of global transformation and healing. As your coaches throughout *Be Like the Wind,* we present our teachings through our special, equine lens.

Connecting with horse power is a direct conduit to your spiritual path.

We three value our role as your spiritual moderators. It is an honor to channel our life stories in the following pages. You will gain perspective through our unique viewpoint, using your spiritual language.

Our messages were transcribed using various methods. Often, it was a direct, spoken communication. Other times we sent a visualization, culminating in a picture that symbolized our meaning. We also communicated via vibration, translating the meaning of our transmissions into words. Vibrational exchanges were affirmed by chills, feathers, wind, and other spiritual signs.

We synergized our energies into one unit, which we named The Triune.

Tasked with a sacred mission, Spirit chose us to coauthor *Be Like the Wind*. A Thoroughbred, an Appendix and a Mustang share our unique life stories to navigate a Divine labyrinth, culminating into this spiritual tome. Our cohesive, unified voice emerged through the following pages, addressing the human condition through a horse's lens.

Nothing was altered from our original transmissions. When modifications were made in the book's wording or style, we orchestrated the changes through telepathic or clairvoyant mediums. The book unfolded according to Divine plan.

Spirit guided us to write our stories in first person. Like a conversation, this style invites a more intimate experience with us. While most readers are familiar with human authors, we convey our thoughts, feelings and emotions in plain language anybody can understand.

We realize reading spiritual messages through our eyes might feel uncomfortable at first. Like a conversation, imagine sharing our innermost desires and sorrows with a dear friend. Throughout the book, our storytelling is honest, grateful, and humble.

Spirit Led the Way

Be Like the Wind's nativity unfolded outside the confines of time and space. Independent of any human thought process, the chapters emerged at their own pace. When they were ready to be birthed, the words lit up like fireflies before your eyes. Spirit led the way.

We often generated new messages into *Be Like the Wind*'s composition. The order of the book changed so many times it made your head spin. You tried and tried to reorganize the chapters with your analytical mind only to discover we created the edits and adaptations, not you!

We guided the process with raw spiritual intelligence.

Trying to force your words on to paper was pointless. It simply confused our core intentions and backfired every time. This book never followed a straightforward path to publication. Once you realized controlling the flow wasn't going to happen according to your outlines and drafts, you surrendered to Spirit, whose directives led the way.

Spirit was the guiding force behind our channeling. We orchestrated every thought form, idea bundling, and execution, yielding the stream of consciousness style we desired. From start to finish, it was out of your hands. Spirit led the way.

Yes, you did select the publishing venue which suited your specific needs. We were behind those choices.

Through and through, Spirit led the way.

Spirit Led the Way

The Language of Spirit

The underlying theme of *Be Like the Wind* is spiritual immersion, growth, and transcendence. Focusing on your soul's Divine truth, we chaperon your thoughts, emotions and actions toward spiritual understanding, connection, and enlightenment.

Our teachings seek to bring light and love into your soul's evolution, uncovering your life's spiritual blueprint.

The written words in *Be Like the Wind* convey pure, absolute energy. Since words carry so much power, we align ourselves with your language, choosing words you comprehend. As your mentors, we desire your spiritual journey be positively imprinted by our messages.

These words transform our telepathic way of communicating energetic symbols into verbal expressions you can comprehend. Transforming our silent way of communicating to a written exchange, you grasp the meanings we intuit. As such, you will understand our intention.

We use the words Divine, Source, Spirit, God, universal consciousness and the oversoul interchangeably to mean the one, omnipresent essence which governs all creation. We also employ your scientific expression for the collective consciousness, the quantum field. Whether you approach the cosmic consciousness from a scientific or spiritual viewpoint, they mean the same thing; all souls are connected to one ever-present unifying force since the beginning of time.

Source is a magnetic power, overseeing the spiritual makeup of the universe. Its creative force touches our physical, emotional, mental, and spiritual layers, including every cell in our bodies.

The Spirit realm also indicates another existing reality beyond the veil, on the other side of life. Spirit can mean your personal, soul signature, or the greater, unified energy. The word Spirit may also mean soul, and vice versa. We may discuss being in Spirit as being no longer in the physical body.

Each one of us is inextricably linked to each other via the Spirit realm. This is a central theme of *Be Like the Wind*. As you read through the following chapters, we encourage you find the vibrational match in our language.

When you find the communicative alignment, it will become your language.

Chapter 2

Spirit Forewarns

The Fire Within

We perceive the emotional fire within and around you. While it manifests to us as a burning energy, it is anger. It is rage. As a race, you consume tremendous amounts of toxic energy which destroys our planet. From the tiniest creatures to the oceans, mountains and atmosphere, the negativity surrounds your physicality, penetrating your energy fields and making you sick.

Your rage is like a volcano ready to erupt at any moment. We feel its heat enflaming and swallowing all life on Earth as you know it. Its explosive nature represents the destruction of your innate good nature, the suppression of Divine creation. On the collective level, many of the positive qualities gifted to humanity have been buried in your wars, your racism, and your social inequities.

Every being on the planet, including the insects, animals, plants, rocks, crystals, and soil fit into the grand design, the universal spiritual matrix of all life. Uniquely designed to play a role in Earth's health and welfare, all creatures deserve to be treated with the same respect and love humans bestow upon one another.

Treating others as if they are lesser creatures does not originate from Source. Too much resentfulness and victimhood govern your beliefs and actions. Blaming others for your own feelings of inadequacy, shame, and guilt will not bring you the inner peace you seek.

The fire within must be calmed, tamed, and extinguished for humanity to heal and the Earth to regenerate. Without this global reversal, the prejudice, warring and killing will be unstoppable. The time is upon you to undertake this enormous task for it is critical for all of mankind.

Be at one with nature and the world. There is grand support from the unseen Spirit realm. The subtle energies surround you, raising your vibration and filling you with love and light. Their sheer presence brings you a greater sense of non-duality and strength, uniting you with the God of your heart.

By connecting to the universal field, this fire will be tamed and extinguished for humanity to heal.

The Human Way

The human way is a solitary one. While your families, friends, acquaintances, and communities provide one level of support and comfort, you must embrace your soul journey alone. This means coming into complete spiritual alignment with yourself. Finding your soul purpose will enhance your decision-making skills, strengthening your connection to the universal consciousness.

To calibrate all aspects of your life, embark on a spiritual journey, accessing your innermost secrets. Digging deep into your roots, your soul yearns for self-discovery and authentication. This deep calling creates profound and permanent healing once you are willing to address your soul healing.

Facing your shadow self is masterful and empowering, clearing out old and toxic energetic patterns. A return to wholeness, your soul journey will unfold and flourish. The unabashed, honest self-searching reveals the truth of who you are and who you are meant to be.

Your Spirit guides and angels have your back. Their support helps you discover, validate, and cherish your connection to the oversoul. Through dedicated spiritual practices, synchronistic life events, dreams, and meditative moments, they provide clear signals. Ask them for help, and they will avail themselves to you.

Your search may or may not flow evenly. Equine energy can be of great assistance because we walk in transparency, honesty, and pure authenticity. Like you, we have our own woundings; despite our imperfections, we do not hide behind the veil and deny what we have to offer.

In contrast, we are willing partners in assisting you with your spiritual growth no matter what type of trauma we have witnessed in our lives. We know your vulnerabilities, your sensitivities, and your secrets. All is safe with us, for we tell no one. We only serve as your guides and allies to bring light to darkness, sadness to joy and pain to release.

Chasing Light

Every creature on Earth is born with a spark of Divine light. Originating from Source, this light resembles a crystal shard, emitting energy into each of your cells. The overflow of spiritual light radiates brightly into your energy field, or aura. Divine light is always shining, regardless of whether you are consciously aware of its presence.

Humans spend lifetimes chasing Divine light. Instead of intuitively embracing it, you search for deep contentment and joy outside of yourself in the external world. Yet, your soul seeks the enlightenment which accompanies deep inner spiritual practice. Thus, you may find it challenging to align your soul with your personal Divine power.

You forget the universal laws of oneness. Believing your physical experience symbolizes your entire life, you eschew your mystical, inner calling. Your physical needs and desires become the guideposts of your existence, closing the connection to Source. Allowing your ego to drive your free will and ultimate choices, you fall prey to greed, anger, frustration, and the ensuing separation from Divine light.

Your inner radiance is inextricably linked to the Divine through intuition and trust. Woven into your entire being, you have access to it every moment throughout your life. Eventually it will manifest as a reflection of the Godlike qualities you are capable of emulating. With spiritual mindfulness and attention, you will start to activate your awareness.

Horses have much to teach you in this realm. We know how to absorb and reflect Divine light, accessing its power to revitalize our energy fields and project it to you. We seek this luminous force to energize our physical bodies. Staying connected to Spirit, all of life's rhythms flow through us. We serve as an energetic conduit, reaching deep into the soul level to correct any imbalances.

Via our soft and gentle manner, we address your authentic, soulful self. Knowing who among you is working on your spiritual journey, we observe and recalibrate your energy and magnetic field. The love vibration alone can bring enormous shifts on the soul level.

We agree via soul contracts to work with you, offering many subtle teachings which activate and transform your life challenges without radical or harmful effects. We invite you to enter our energy fields, where we track and acknowledge any transparency or false sense of self. There we easily discern who is connected to Spirit.

We are available to assist you to generate these changes. Allow us into your soul, opening to the field of infinite possibilities, the quantum.

Divine light is something you need not hunt because it is already contained in your soul. Chasing light only leads to isolation and loneliness, a void in time and space. Our invitation is open, awaiting a call to action in this most essential life mission. Only a breath away, spiritual light is readily accessible.

Climbing the Mountain

Achievement is a big word in your human world. Like climbing a mountain, much of your life is spent attempting to accomplish more, crafting your self-defining beliefs according to societal valuations. Whether it is your career, your relationships, the money you accumulate, or your possessions, these appear to be the barometers of success.

Once you have reached the summit, you feel you've accomplished a great feat. But then there is a second, a third and a fourth mountain. The bar keeps getting higher and higher. Your sense of self is often inextricably linked to external measures of advancement.

You seek gratification from temporary and superficial landmarks, ignoring the inner calling of your soul. Somehow the deep satisfaction isn't there because you covet energy rather than being of service to the Spirit realm. Unheard, the voice of your soul will continue to knock at your door until it is recognized.

Your soul purpose yearns to awaken, nudging you to go within. You do not need to be something bigger or better than your fellow man because it is all about the conscious connection to your Source. On this level of universal consciousness, we are unified as one; there is no division among man or beast and the oversoul.

There are no judgments or assessments in the Spirit world. Your accomplishments or societal status are not calculated or tallied for your soul's ascendance. On the contrary, walking the Spirit path opens your eyes to the infinite realm where magic, manifestation and profound changes materialize.

Horses approach life very differently. Once our survival needs of food, shelter, water and procreation of our species are addressed, we place ourselves in your service, shepherding you to become the best version of yourselves. Partnering with you is invaluable, for we deeply desire to please.

We serve mankind to raise your spiritual vibration, connecting you to the eternal Divine energy. As conduits to the unseen realms, we invite you to cross this bridge with us and discover this wonderment. There you will interface at the everlasting level where infinite love and goodness abound.

When you are climbing the mountain, seek to access the Spirit realm's infinite possibilities. Bringing internal bliss, Spirit's love is the most important aspect of your lives.

Allow us into your personal space to guide you beyond the mountaintops.

Climbing the Mountain

The Why

For centuries, you have turned to religion, science, and spirituality to comprehend the order of the universe, the origins of suffering, and why bad things happen to good people. You attempt to explain the origins of wars, conflict, and human frailty. Digging deep in history, you search precedents, evidence, and patterns to interpret your human condition and its complexities.

You seek answers to the issues and problems in your own lives. Since your challenges may be passed from lifetime to lifetime, many of you live in perpetuity, continually chasing solutions you believe to be true. What you may be seeking is often right before your eyes, buried deep inside your soul.

While being sagacious may help shape your decisions, it does not necessarily control the desired outcomes. Rather, seeking closure can have the opposite effect, enabling you to behave in an entitled, self-serving fashion instead of focusing on the greater good.

On the contrary, your soul's spiritual contract from birth to death is the primary factor circumscribing your Spirit path. Implementing your free will allows you to make changes according to your life experiences. This is the principle of allowing and letting go of outcomes. It creates great freedom in your life.

For us, it doesn't matter to us whether we know the answers or not. We were not born to solve problems or provide answers but just to be horses plain and simple. We master the flow of life, allowing our individual life plan to unfold.

We live in the moment. The power of "now" supersedes the grand human search surrounding you. In a millisecond, the now holds the possibility of choice, which determines how you think and behave. In turn your energy will follow your thoughts, creating greater awareness for change and growth. Thus, answers to the "whys" in your human race lie in the present moment where all your power resides.

Since part of our job on Earth is to serve you, we seek to do this in the most loving way possible. We aspire to be those who appreciate this quality of our essence. Our goal is co-creating partnerships with equanimity, patience, respect, and most of all, love. Without these attributes, our relationships with you are meaningless.

Do not seek to answer all your life questions. There may not be answers in your physical world. Simply live your life in complete authenticity and walk the Spirit path, where you will discover the answers you need.

Letting go of the Why is a huge release.

Chapter 3

Spirit Appoints

The Eminent Horse

As creatures of physical grandeur, speed, endurance and perseverance, equines present as very powerful beings. Since the acquisition of power has been an ongoing human priority, we have been your steady comrades in this mission. Our species has enabled you to expand your global economic and political governorships.

Throughout history, no other animal has given you the freedom of mobility like the horse. We assisted you to become impressive, mounted warriors and soldiers. We are your conduits to all peoples across the continents.

No matter what role you assign to us, we accept our responsibilities with grace and dignity. Our bravery is unsurpassed. We will prove our loyalty to you in any situation you present to us. Whether carrying you into battle, or faithfully serving as farm, racing or performance horses, we epitomize the essence of freedom, stamina, and strength.

A unique energy, horse power assists your Spirit path. By sharing it with you, your own strength develops. Using your free will, you find your innate wisdom and trust to find answers to your queries.

Horse power can be used on many levels; yet, it should not be used in a negative fashion, abused, wasted or kept to ourselves. At the ego level, power may be used for personal gain, with complete disregard of others' needs. At worst it may be used at the cost of others. As there are misuses of power to be seen and found all around us, those on the Spirit path frequently have negative emotions toward it.

But being powerless is not the answer either. You must learn to use power correctly. Sharing your power with others and showing them how to develop their power speeds up your journey and makes it more joyful. This is an important lesson to learn, and horse is your charismatic teacher.

As your dynamic coaches, we urge you to use your power correctly, blending your inner and outer worlds. Finding balance in your own inherent strength is key to reserving your power when it is called for. With practice, you will learn to conserve or wield your personal power for the purpose of the greater good.

Like the horse, you can preserve your power until it is called forth as a demonstration of courage and fortitude. Harmonized with your Divine blueprint, your spiritual growth will flourish. You will discover the roots of true power, emerging from the depths of your soul.

Our real, true power lies within our ability to move through our physical, emotional, and mental challenges with great inner strength.

The Intuitive Horse

Horses are supremely psychic creatures. Our super-sensory abilities are a legacy, dating back to the time of Alexander the Great. His famous horse, Bucephalus, was one of the most ascended equine masters of his day. He taught Alexander how to read, feel and emanate energy into their relationship.

Horses were soon elevated to a new status as companions and warriors. You can find our stories in any historical records. There are many accounts of kings, knights, queens, and other heroes whose relationship with their horse went above and beyond the confines of ordinary life.

We read your mind. Before you recognize a thought entering your consciousness, it was transmitted to ours. The thought left your conscious mind long before you knew it. When we react, we have already received your transmission.

Like you, we are sentient beings. We experience the full spectrum of our emotions, shaping our life experiences. An advanced consciousness, our ability to read and interpret your energy has tailored us into supreme facilitators for spiritual transcendence. Our highly developed consciousness enables us to coexist with you.

Our intuitive gifts are identical with our predecessors. We strive to share these gifts with you, especially those of you who understand what we see, hear and project into your reality. Once you recognize our abilities, your perception will shift from a one-dimensional to a multidimensional viewpoint.

As highly psychic animals, we sense the unseen realm, serving as your bridge to the Spirit world.

Supreme Beings of Light

Horses embody the ancestral codes given to us during the time of creation. Some of the material is genetic DNA; other codes represent our own unique lexicon. These light-filled emissions cultivated and enriched our historic horse-human relationships, evolving into a grand matrix linked to the quantum field.

Gifted by Spirit to hold light for all humanity, the equine ancestry is a source of Divine essence.

Our light codes enliven your path. When activated, these dynamic light rays transfer from horse to human. Perfected through our intra-species spiritual awareness and growth, we evolved into supreme beings of light. As your loyal companions, we are ready to dispatch our missives. It is our duty to channel this original spark into present time, for the benefit of all mankind.

As your teachers, we endeavor to project our magnetic energy, strength, and stamina to you, illuminating your path with the great light we bear.

Chapter 4

Forming the Triune

The Equine Council of Elders

Equine ancestry follows the guidelines of universal law. These covenants circumscribe how horses and humans have coexisted since the beginning of time, shaping equine destiny from the time of the Eohippus to the present. A spiritual knowingness, these laws are to be immutable.

Along this timeline, the Equine Council of Elders was formed. The Council represents a group of highly ascended beings who have spent many lifetimes as a horse. Some members of the Council lived as unicorns; others embodied different equine forms throughout the ages. Most of the Council members reincarnated hundreds of lifetimes as your companions, servants, warhorses and more.

In the last few hundred years, the Equine Council instituted a plan to educate humans in spiritual law. There are millions of you who walk path with us, though many of you are not yet consciously aware of our coaching. It is an evolving process, one that has accelerated with the arrival of the fifth dimensional energy.

The spiritual directive borne by the Council is vast and all encompassing. Its primary role is intelligence, a specific guidance in the form of horse-human kinship. Here is what the Equine Council has to say: "For centuries, we have initiated deep karmic agreements with you. Horse power and strength cannot be underestimated because our collective essence represents the earth, fire, water, and air elements. We offer these attributes to you during this time of great evolutionary change, revealing universal spiritual teachings as a service to humanity."

The Council chose three horses to step forth and communicate their messages to you. Unique in their missions and relationships to the human they served, they bring forth their narratives. Carrying words of Divine wisdom, grace, trust and unconditional love, their transmissions became the bedrock for a book about the love humans share with horses.

The Equine Council was the motivating force behind Be Like the Wind's creation.

If this is your first introduction to horse talk, please understand all species are just as proficient as we are in communicating with humans. While dogs, cats and other companion animals may be more accessible to you, horses have an extraordinary ability to calm your soul and assist in your energetic healing. Therefore, we encourage you to spend time in our physical presence, receiving the true authentic power we offer.

The Power of Three

The number three is an integral part of *Be Like the Wind*. Woven throughout the book, we three horses formed a union from start to finish, arranging every detail from our synchronous meetups to our soul contracts and journeys to the Spirit world. Linked to the Trinity, the number three is quite spiritual, featuring innumerable messages.

Three is a triad, containing a beginning, middle and end. Like *Be Like the Wind*'s progression, there is a clear start, ascent, and lastly a deeper exploration into the Spirit world. The journey began with one horse, ending with a triage of three.

Not coincidentally, the element of three is historically considered a sacred-like oneness. By virtue of its very properties and particular attributes, three is seen throughout Biblical texts and spiritual writings. The triad seals the union of oneness and separation; from this primordial triangle all figures derive.

One of *Be Like the Wind*'s main themes is the non-duality of all creation. Part of the whole, three also represents the tripartite nature of the world. Mother Earth is composed of three elements: water, heaven, and sky.

Eliciting a euphonious feeling, the trinity exudes balance, harmony, and peace. Its components are eternally connected, highlighting the connection between past, present, and future or mind, body, and spirit. In its composition, each triage section points outward, indicating a correlation to the infinite, impermanent nature of the universe.

Three is an inclusive number, symbolizing the "all." Representing completion and contentment, the power of three is a central theme in *Be Like the Wind*. Three is a symbol of something solid, real, significant, and complete. An emblem of spiritual significance, three appears in everything exceptional.

Omniscience, Omnipresence and Omnipotence are God's characteristics.

The Power of Three

The Triune

We have been together in four previous lifetimes. During the passage of time, we collaborated to assist all of humanity at a convergent moment. To do so, we selected a human horse whisperer as the means to achieve our goal.

We three horses come forward as one entity, a spiritual triune. Speaking collectively in the following chapters, we speak as one entity. Light filled, all our individual experiences are woven together into one beautiful tapestry, infusing it with Divine timing and grace.

As one unified voice, we call ourselves The Triune.

Over the course of 20 years, our collective mission unfolded. Channeling our stories and messages, our communiqués were woven into masterful language. Cultivated into a written format, their spiritual applications provide relevant information for our fellow travelers.

Be Like the Wind features the significance of our personal journeys, offering a myriad of spiritual messages. Through these life perspectives, you will hear our advice about love, kinship, mastery and transformation. We hope you will recover hope and renewal for all of mankind.

Some of the spiritual teachings gathered in *Be Like the Wind* were conveyed while we lived on the earth plane; others were sent from the Spirit realm. There is an order to when and how we conveyed them. We intend our voices to reverberate through the quantum, benefitting all living beings on Earth.

Taking time to savor the details about Spirit-to-Spirit communication, these chapters endeavor to open new healing pathways. Emphasizing the transformative power of Source, we hope you discover its magic and wonderment. It is our deepest desire you pursue a deep personal bond with the Spirit world, fostering healthy partnerships with one another while reaching greater states of enlightenment and peace.

The teachings offered by The Triune are universal, and timeless.

Our Offering

As Gaia ushers in a period of global transformation, time is of the essence to step forth and offer our messages to you. We have been waiting for the convergence of these earthly energies to present these spiritual truths to you. Our unified voice imports the vibrational scope required to effect these changes.

From one of the most ancient earthly creatures to the modern horse, equine ancestral evolution has enabled us to refine our communication skills with you. Centuries of service to mankind perfected our highly developed intuition. Unlike any other creature whose mission is to serve, heal and transform, horses have forged an implacable bond with you.

Because we are strongly grounded to the Earth, horses convey an enormous amount of energy from their physical bodies into the quantum field. Connecting our energetic bodies with yours, we merge our individual fields. Once our energies are blended, you can feel the safety net and healing potential we propose.

Being in our company alone can transport you across the veil into the Spirit realm. A transformational experience, we augment our messages and stories to demonstrate the sheer dynamism of our horse-human relationships. While other members of the Spirit world endorse your life mission, horse talk is straightforward and easy to assimilate. Your personal guides, angels, nature spirits, animals, and minerals also present unlimited opportunities for enlightenment.

Our offering is limitless, unbound by the physical earthly dimensions.

Our Mission

Why did the Equine Council choose the three of us? We were chosen for several reasons. First, we are sentient beings, like all living creatures. As such, we share the same emotions, feelings, and trauma as you do. We understand your life challenges of abuse, abandonment, and healing, in a parallel fashion to ours.

Second, we observe and feel the anger in your human race. As your historical partners, we have watched how you chase spiritual light rather than cultivating your own internal Spiritual tools for Divine guidance. We recognize your solitary way, fashioning non-dual relationships with all of creation rather than finding peace in Divine oneness.

Most importantly, we are supremely connected to you through our psychic abilities. Clairvoyant, clairsentient, and clairaudient, we can broadcast and receive your thoughts telepathically no matter whether we are present. Our loyal and courageous spirit enables you to achieve limitless accomplishments, therefore becoming your trusted advisors and companions with our insights.

Now it is time for us to speak up, bringing forth our spiritual inspirations.

Why now? There is no better time than the present to raise global spiritual awareness. As your beloved partners, we witness extreme human suffering. Observing your worldly chaos, we desire to participate in its healing.

Use *Be Like the Wind* as your spiritual teaching guide. Intuit how we serve as your mentors and role models. Implant our advice in your own lives by relying on the grounding and strength we bring into our relationships with you. Whether or not you have ever felt our true majestic presence and healing energy, we believe you will find meaning in our communiques.

Part II

The Triune Collaborates

Chapter 5

Three Divine Principles

Spirit selected three Divine principles to silhouette our channelings. Divine order, guidance and grace consistently emerged throughout the following chapters, gently affirming how our spiritual journey unfolded. Using your mind as a helpful organizational tool, your conscious thoughts surrendered to the book's Divine flow when you struggled with the inevitable roadblocks along the way.

Divine Order

A strategy was planned long before you were born. Contractual in nature, your Divine blueprint was written to introduce we three horses precisely when the moment arrived. Therefore, a firm spiritual mandate became clear with the passage of linear time.

The amalgamation was formed long before you met us.

In Divine order, we entered your life one by one, aligning our souls with yours. The soul merger was preplanned. Perfectly orchestrated to blend with horses from your birth forward, we stepped forth when the alliance was primed for success. It was Divinely ordained and blessed by the Equine Council, signaling the progression followed a spiritual order.

Even though we shared separate past lives with you, this lifetime was different. According to a grand scheme, your soul's evolution merged with ours. This coupling enabled a deeper psychic connection than previous incarnations.

Spirit planned to release our stories for all mankind according to a calibrated order and plan.

Divine Guidance

Like every human, your Spirit team guides your life experiences. What might appear to be coincidental, is not. Every event in your life correlates with a metaphysical message indicating a spiritual attunement is taking place on the soul level. Nothing is random, even the most terrifying or glorifying moments. Believing these principles is critical for a deep-rooted connection to the universal field.

This is Divine law.

Divine guidance surrounds you all the time. All of life's blessings, joys, traumas, and sorrows reflect Spirit's teachings, helping you reach a state of complete alignment with Source. Angels, ancient ancestors, nature spirits or animal companions are present in your energy field. Tailored to your specific wishes and desires, your personal Spirit team members have your back.

Accessing advice from the Spirit world is as simple as opening a conversation with your dearest friend.

Like you, horses are Divinely protected and guided. From birth, we receive the teachings of our elders, our parents, our grandparents, and other ancient lineages. We have our own guardian angels who keep us safe while we travel the earthly plane.

Helping humans perceive Divine guidance is one of our deepest desires. Conveying these subtle messages to you is part of our mission on Earth. As your spiritual allies, we wish to share this knowledge with you, cultivating your own navigation tools in the Spirit realm.

Divine Grace

A state of heightened vibration, Divine grace is a fusion of intention, will, choice and manifestation. A sublime metaphysical state, grace converges earthly and spiritual energies. Grace manifests when a grand spiritual alignment is materializing in a complete energetic immersion.

Grace produces resilience, a strong resolve, and an unshakable connection to the Divine. It emboldens a complete and trustful relationship with all other beings. It is omnipresent, purifying and beautifying for your soul. When grace is bestowed upon you, it is unmistakably clear you have received a Divine blessing.

An infinite energy from the unified field of consciousness, grace is a regenerative force.

Divine grace imparts a desired state of being. A sincere commitment to spiritual practice will enable its presence. Whether this is achieved through prayer, meditation, yoga or a fundamental belief system, engagement with your core beliefs will activate a state of grace.

Divine grace reveals the quantum reality of your universe.

While you are born with a spark of the Divine, it can take lifetimes to develop and refine your core beliefs, devotion, and faith required to master a state of grace. Seeking the answers from Spirit, grace will bring clarity to your life's challenges. With ongoing patience and devotion, each of you can reach this plane of consciousness, uniting your soul with the Divine.

Horses are infused with Divine grace. You see it in our eyes, the windows of our soul. We reflect a luminous spark in our countenance, shining brightly from the inside out. Aligned with pure, universal natural law, we radiate peace, calmness, bliss, light, sound, energy, and wisdom.

We recognize this same quality in you when you live in a state of grace. It is our spiritual responsibility to bridge the Divine and physical realms, absorbing sacred light and unconditional love. Transmuting this light to humanity, we share Divine love in your presence, conjoining us in a state of inspiration, strength, and Divine grace.

A moment of fusion, Divine order, guidance, and grace coalesced when you met me, Billy.

Divine Order

Chapter 6

Our Spiritual Contracts

Billy

Billy: I was the Initiator, chosen by the Equine Council to jumpstart your spiritual awakening. My capricious and humorous personality invited joy and play into our relationship. You found my lighthearted attitude endearing. I was so different than any horse you had ever encountered, providing the means for spiritual exploration and tutorship.

The awakening came in stages along your linear timeline, taking you from your childhood to the present moment. Each step along the way was purposefully directed toward an apex when we met. All your life experiences to date were activated when you and I became partners.

I was the conduit for spiritual initiation.

A magnanimous personality, my sense of humor channeled in a completely new energy to you. It was a refreshing, captivating experience, one which delighted and surprised you.

Embarking on a new course in equine partnership, I selected an innovative approach, sheer play. Through play and telepathic communication, our relationship evolved seamlessly.

With me, you had permission to be yourself. Partnering with a horse did not have to carry heavy duties and responsibilities. I did not take anything seriously, so mistakes were not part of my repertoire. You were permitted to unfold as a spiritual being, letting loose of who you were in relation to THE HORSE.

Being with me felt like you were back in kindergarten.

I opened your conscious mind to a world of unlimited possibilities and wonderment. Eventually, as I joined Monty and Romeo in the Triune, our teachings all made sense. Our synchronous arrivals in your life were preordained, a progression of soul agreements according to Spirit's master plan. You gained a deeper understanding of why I was "the initiator."

Generating the Divine spark within you, our soul agreement was an activation of spiritual light and love.

Monty

Monty: I was the Psychic Connector, matching your level of sensitivity. Our vibrational resonance gave you immediate feedback on the impact of your own thoughts and feelings. A two-way communication between us, our telepathic exchanges were dynamic.

With synchronous precision, my arrival was also foreordained. We met when both of us were experiencing prolonged trauma. You were healing up a shoulder from a horse accident. I was stuck in a cycle of recurring physical stressors. When our paths crossed, something clicked in your consciousness.

While a bit rocky at the start, I took over the main task of blending our souls. You intuited what was happening because of our parallel sensitivities. It was an exciting process, reading each other's minds and sensing the vibrations between us.

I came into your life when both of us were dealing with fear.

You did not feel safe on horseback and knew your fear was transferring to me. While you did not recognize it right away, my fears of men, new situations, bicycles, public parks and even trailering heightened your awareness of how vulnerable I felt. Identifying with me opened the pathway to examine your own feelings. At times the fear was so intense in my body you picked up on it, making yourself even more nervous. Facing it square on, you considered quitting the sport altogether.

We reflected our anxieties back and forth, acknowledging it was time to resolve them. Releasing these pervasive fears together helped calm our emotions. Your love for me helped me move beyond my traumatic memories.

A loving energy empowered our spiritual agreement, helping us release the past.

Your continual encouragement and support made a big difference to me, especially when I had reached my tolerance point and could not stand certain situations for more than a few minutes. As I became more and more confident, my emotions stabilized.

Thus, our soul agreement was to move through fear into a trusting and joyful relationship.

Romeo

Romeo: I am the Love Ambassador. I reflect the ultimate healing power of unconditional love physically, emotionally, mentally, and spiritually. I am your heart horse, through and through.

The information I shared about my capture and prison life moved you deeply. Acknowledging the scars from my time in captivity facilitated an unshakable bond between us. My complete metamorphosis was a result of the love we share from the heart.

I continue to embellish this alignment, bestowing its finishing touches. Since I engage my soul from a place of unconditional love, it is easy to perceive our abiding, infinite connection. It is an evolution, enabling both of us to feel our spiritual engagement.

At the time of this writing, you and I continue our soul journey together. You have witnessed a complete transformation in our relationship. The more love you express to me, the deeper the alliance becomes. Living from a loving space continues to enhance your spiritual development.

The power of love symbolizes the soul agreement between us.

Spoken as the Triune: "Given our diverse backgrounds, a preplanned, synchronistic flow unfolded as we came into your life. As members of your Spirit team, we accompany you each step of the way. Endorsing the power of our soul-to-soul contracts, it was our earnest and forthright dedication to scribe *Be Like the Wind*. A Divine plan was inaugurated, a contract to scribe *Be Like the Wind*."

Chapter 7

I Am Billy, a Thoroughbred

I was born on a thoroughbred breeding farm in Tennessee. Descending from a well-known lineage of show horses from France, England and Italy, my grandparents and parents were champion hunter-jumpers, dressage, and conformation horses. These strong bloodlines produced proud and beautiful equines.

With near perfect conformation, I was a standout young colt. An eye-catching youngster, I was pure black with only a few white markings on my legs and forehead. These stunning characteristics molded me into a conformation show horse. Imagine being so handsome, I was judged by my legs, hips, neck, head, and overall structure. I was a horse model!

Fortunately, my early profession as a conformation horse spared me the racetrack. I know my gentle nature would have been destroyed by the fierce competition there. I was always a bit clumsy because of my front left club foot, so I would have tripped and hurt myself at a young age.

After my conformation wins, I went on to hunter-jumper training. The competition was challenging and intense. I excelled at the sport, making me a great candidate for the show circle. I was only three years old and 16.2 hands tall.

My owners entered me in many shows, where I became a champion. I won countless blue ribbons, delighting my humans. Being a playful fellow, I enjoyed sailing over the jumps and galloping around the arena. I felt vibrant and young while my riders rejoiced.

I had numerous homes, each one more lavish than the previous one. Even though I excelled at my sport, I hadn't found the satisfaction of being with a human. My owners were young riders, seeking adventure while hoping to gain glory and recognition from the momentary pleasure in the winners' circle.

As fate would have it, I ended up in a boarding barn in Florida, where I was used as a lesson horse. Feeling disconnected from all the different people who came to ride me, I was deeply unhappy with this job. I showed my displeasure by bucking them off, one by one.

Hoping to make money from me, the owners put me up for sale again. I felt sad I'd be rehomed to another barn where I didn't belong, nor be appreciated. My deepest desire was to find a human who understood and valued me.

The saving grace for me was my whimsical personality. Due to my fancy and pampered upbringing, I sized up every human from top to bottom. I loved to make people laugh with my quirky sense of humor. I was quite confident; it took a bold rider to keep up with me or I would happily dump him.

My behavior kept many from getting to know me, but once we bonded, I became your best friend for life.

Our Meetup

After your family moved to Florida, you felt an urge to find a stable where you could ride a couple times each week. Yearning to rekindle your relationship with horses, the pull was strong and persistent. Many years later you realized it was the genesis of your spiritual awakening.

You had no clue the entire expedition was preordained by Spirit.

Searching around for places to ride, you found me at a boarding barn. It was recently renovated, and the owners were very accommodating. When you called upon them, there I stood, waiting to meet you.

A beautiful, big black thoroughbred. Dumbfounded, the look on your face expressed complete amazement. Standing still on the crossties, you were not expecting such a regal creature to look you straight in the eye. I caught you completely off guard!

I was the most magnificent horse you had ever seen. Tall and shiny, my essence was noble. You had never encountered a horse with such an aristocratic presence; yet, despite my extraordinary appearance, you recognized the humility I bore in my heart.

My soft, quiet eyes spoke volumes about the depth of my soul. I put you on edge, disclosing I could read your mind. Your intuition told you I already knew everything about you.

While you assumed being an equine beauty queen might have flattered my ego, my earthy attitude was captivating. Caring nothing about my fancy, papered breeding, you were mesmerized by my outgoing, bold character. My curious and proud personality did not offend you; instead, you wanted to learn everything about me.

Within two minutes of our meetup, one of the barn owners walked over and told you I had a special trick. "Watch," she said. She touched the end of my nose and tickled it. Then I proceeded to stick out my tongue, standing there like a big dog. My tongue hung down, begging for a scratch.

This huge sense of humor was unlike anything you'd ever encountered. Who knew horses could stick their tongue out "on cue"? I had a smile on my face, watching your complete amazement.

Smitten by my energy, my inquisitiveness captured all your senses.

You burst into laughter. Impressed with my intelligence, you stood there pondering how I made you laugh so easily. I had already seduced you with my goofy trick, so you were intrigued to see what I felt like under saddle.

Highly trained, I was one of the most comfortable horses you'd ever ridden. I was sensitive and responsive to your cues. One slight leg aid told me to change pace, moving from a trot to a canter or lead change. With incredibly smooth gaits, I was a sheer joy to ride.

You were ecstatic. It was as if you were floating on a cloud. There was something beyond horse and rider blend you could not identity. Not realizing I was your first spiritual mentor, you knew we had already forged a marvelous partnership.

Years later you realized it was our Divine connection.

I was the second horse you had ever "owned," so you were brand new at horse keeping. The boarding barn took care of my feed, turnout, and medical care. You were responsible for my training, and fitness. There was much to learn, and you embraced the challenge willingly.

It was a very exciting time for you although you were a busy mom with three kids under the age of six. You carved out our quality time when they were in school or brought them along to experience our rewarding interactions.

It was a magical and life-changing phase of your life.

You and I became fast friends. You decided I was the perfect companion, knowing in your heart we'd been together in many previous lifetimes. You intuited our liaison was Divinely ordained because we were embarking on a spiritual path together.

Like two best friends, we spent many hours goofing around and getting to know each other. You liked to ride the trails alone, something I was not crazy about. I would protest at the gate when you tried to take me out solo but riding with other horses was acceptable. Occasionally I would acquiesce, carrying you out in the open space, where the two of us could run through the sand and let our cares fly with the wind.

And so, our 14-year relationship unfolded. Each day brought different adventures, and we began to know one another's personalities and how to interact as two compatible spirits. I finally felt loved and cherished for being me, all of me.

I was a content and happy fellow, realizing I had finally found my human.

The Initiation

The Equine Council chose me as your first teacher because of your life's timing. Surrounded my own team of Spirit guides, I was up for the task. An honoring, it was Divinely ordained. The moment we met, we embarked on a sacred path together.

I was your first spiritual coach.

How was I to begin with a human? I had no idea what I was being asked to do. But the first time I met you, I knew it was going to be easy. And fun.

Unsure about how to teach you, I took it slowly. I began by giving you soft nudges with my nose. I made frequent eye contact, holding you in my energy field. I made it clear I was your soul mate, supercharging our encounters with tremendous laughter and fun.

Drawn to my personality and tricks, these outward symbols magnetized you to my aura. You were the perfect candidate for spiritual initiation. Nonetheless, you were unsuspecting your life was about to change in a big way.

By way of synchronicity, you were completely open and receptive to the Spirit-Spirit connection. On a deeper level, your soul was searching for our spiritual connection. With your enthusiasm, I was able to introduce quantum principles into your consciousness. Once our bond was set, the telepathic messages were easily transmitted.

Curious about horses as sentient beings, your childlike energy was pure and unfiltered. Your soul was opening to the magic and intrigue you felt around me, eager to absorb Divine information. Our relationship was different than any of your previous ones, but you had yet to recognize the subtle shift in consciousness I was orchestrating.

Your excitement for our partnership was invigorating. While neoteric, the spiritual seed had germinated. I could see the spark in your eyes, which made me feel elated.

Designated as your very first spiritual mentor, I chose the light of play as our interactive energy.

The Light of Play

Play is a free-flowing and expansive energy. It redirects your self-critical feelings and actions into a more relaxed and untethered arena. Play is a light-filled art form, galvanizing more joy, happiness, and flexibility in your life.

According to my teachings, this version of play was invigorating. I mean a "goofing around" type of play, exclusive of our riding style or achievements. My goal was eye-to-eye laughter and fun. We did this in several ways.

In a mindful fashion, we took long walks around the barn property. You observed which of the other horses caught my attention, and how I interacted with them. You gave me a bath to see whether I liked the water and scrubbing. To your delight, I loved the attention and care.

Our energies were synched in a playful container.

Our riding adventures began slowly. First it was a simple workout around the arena. When you added jumps to our routine, I lived up to my champion reputation. A good fit, I didn't try to buck you off, not once.

Pretty soon we ventured out on the trail in a group, an activity I enjoyed. I wasn't as spooky as you might have imagined. It was a relaxing time together, with play our motivation.

Dressage lessons brought in another level of play, generating a new version of unity. Engaging as novices, I taught you to enjoy your lessons, focusing on fun rather than performance. My smooth and comfortable rhythms centered and grounded both of us, achieving oneness.

Dressage training was a spiritual experience.

Full of adventure, our kinship grew into a lasting relationship. A period of transformation, I gently introduced you to many important lessons. Through my tutorship, you gained a different perspective on life, impermanence and more.

Play is very important in the Spirit world because it invites participation from your guides, angels, and nature spirits. Helping create your life's experiences, these invisible forces initiate your desires. Since they manifest in a lighthearted and cheerful fashion, you recognize it is they who bring in the light of play.

A buoyant, enthusiastic energy, play opens the portals to the Spirit realm.

The Wake-Up Call

Do you remember the day your father died? An unexpected call from your brother told you he had taken his life, leaving you in a state of complete shock. Although you knew his health was declining rapidly, his suicide happened suddenly, immediately after your last phone conversation with him.

Your offer to care for him was rejected. He refused to join you and your family, shutting out any end-of-life care you might have provided. He wanted no one by his side when he left this world.

It transpired exactly as he wished.

I knew immediately a crisis had occurred. Your energy field was gray, and sluggish. There was no smile on your face, nor any joy in your presence. And then I intuited your father had died, all alone with no one by his side.

You were confused and heartbroken, wondering what else might have been done to help him at the end of his life. Explaining the situation to me, you didn't understand why he would not allow you to visit him in another city or say goodbye before he died. This was a difficult time for you.

Completely unprepared for his swift demise, you found yourself searching for answers. Trying to find some semblance of closure around his unfortunate circumstances, you came to the barn seeking companionship and comfort. Your grief was palpable.

As always, you could count on me to cheer you up. I was primed for the wake-up call.

The rules were rewritten that day. Saddled up and ready to go, I was eager to support you. Rather than protest at the gate, we exited the barn property without any hassle. I made my intentions perfectly clear about the path we were to embark upon. My willingness to comply caught you off guard, but a ride in the wildlife sanctuary was just what you needed.

Off we went, alone on the long, sandy trail. I carried you silently while your emotions rolled out of your heart into a steady stream of tears. Realizing I had previously refused to leave the property alone, you knew something different had just transpired.

A day of awakening unfolded. Activated by a telepathic exchange, a call to Spirit materialized. Your soul recalibrated to an entirely new energy, one where my voice became an integral part of our relationship. The confluence of events was Divinely ordained, the beginning of your sacred evolution.

A prescient moment the day your father died, it was a revered decree, an opening to the Spirit world.

The Move

When your children were old enough to enter the higher grades, your family moved to Colorado. The Florida climate was wearing on you, impelling you to seek a more seasonal lifestyle. I was ready to leave the oppressive summer heat and mosquitos. Besides, I would follow you anywhere you went.

I was sent ahead of your family while you organized your move and packed up your home. I traveled across the country for three full days in a semi-load trailer. I was comfortable and well taken care of, so I made the trip in great shape.

It took a few months for you to relocate, so I was boarded in a local barn. While it was a bit lonely for me, I anticipated a brand new lifestyle with new friends and adventures. I patiently awaited your arrival.

Finally, you built a wonderful barn on the side of a hill with a big twelve-acre pasture. I loved the cool weather and bug-free climate. This was heaven on Earth. I eagerly hoped others were joining me to fill the two stalls.

Montana's arrival was one of my most vivid memories. He came in the dead of winter, a bag of skin and bones. While I could sense he was quite traumatized, we became instant friends. An auspicious juncture in our plan for the Triune, his life had been spared by your decision to remove him swiftly from a downward spiraling situation.

Like me, Monty was a sensitive one, so we bonded immediately. Knowing Spirit had orchestrated our meeting, our relationship was easy and strong. The little gray quarter horse was angry, chasing me around the pasture. She was very jealous of my swift friendship with Monty, but eventually we three worked it out.

Life in Colorado was never dull. You brought horse ladies to ride me, exploring the woods and fields all over the neighborhood. You had many friends, and I got along well with their horses. As a steady and calm older horse, I could carry most riders confidently so they could relax and enjoy themselves as we explored the many nearby trails and parks.

What a different lifestyle from the Florida hurricanes and floods! It was a relief to live in a cozy barn with access to plenty of fresh grass and flowers during the summer season. The cold winters didn't bother me because we had heavy, waterproof blankets protecting us from the snow and rain.

A new chapter in our lives, the move to Colorado facilitated a different lifestyle. Monty's arrival signaled the second step in your spiritual transformation. The symbiotic force guiding our energetic agreements was rapidly shifting.

The provenance for The Triune's strategy was revealed.

Passing the Spiritual Baton to Monty

When Montana arrived at our Colorado barn, I was completely shocked. I had never witnessed such starvation and abuse in my life. My heart broke for this comrade whose will to live had almost expired. You saved his life just in time.

He gradually gained weight and began to trust. I gave him my full and unconditional reassurance, encouraging him to eat and absorb the love available from our human. It would take time to prepare him to be next in line as your teacher. In the meantime, we spent quality time together cavorting about in the lovely pastures we lovingly called horse heaven.

One year later, Monty began to recuperate from the deep trauma of his past. He had hope.

This period coincided with my physical demise. As my body began to break down, it was perfect timing to pass my spiritual baton to Monty. Spirit worked quietly to move parts of my soul into his. This intimate, co-creative transition was unfolding in the subtle realm.

You had no idea how sensitive Monty was. Although you knew he was profoundly wounded, you had not witnessed his psychic abilities. As I helped him with his confidence, his extrasensory skills began to flourish.

Monty's capacity for telepathic communication was extraordinary. His sixth sense was highly attuned to Spirit. His clairvoyant skills were quite advanced. Due to his high level of perception, teaching him how to relate to a sensitive human was a captivating experience.

He already knew everything. Like a novel on a dusty shelf in an old, historic library, it needed a brush off. The guidance I was providing was simply a recap of his soul's previous experiences.

You and Monty formed a strong bond, unwinding the fear and shock of his experiences. Monty gave you plenty of practice time with your new energy tools. His physical and emotional healing were clear signs a great transformation was taking place in both of you, an empowerment reaching far into the metaphysical dimension.

Slowly but surely, Monty regained his zest for life along with his trust of the humans who deeply loved and cared for him.

My last interaction with Monty was the touchstone of success. It was my time to leave, so I said my goodbyes knowing my trip to the vet would be my last. In a poignant moment, Monty told me he understood he was taking my place as your mentor. I reassured him he was primed. His body had healed, and his emotional state was now open to adventure with our human. He valued how cherished he felt, knowing unequivocally your dedication to his well-being superseded any of his past concerns.

He was ready. Our souls had merged into one unit.

My Trip to the Spirit World

As I entered my twenties, I was ready to retire. I was too stiff to enjoy the steep hills and long rides. In my last year of life, I experienced five bouts of colic, each one a little more serious than the previous one.

Varying in severity, two colic episodes required overnight stays at the veterinary clinic where they pumped me full of fluids and anti-inflammatory medicines. During one memorable visit, you and your colleagues performed energy work on me for three full hours while the staff watched us on camera from the front office.

For a moment in time, my life was spared.

The day I transitioned to the Spirit realm started off quietly except I was off my feed. Concerned, you called your vet, who came to our barn at 10 a.m. He was not worried about me because my gums were pink, so he did not think I was having another episode of colic.

While you two chatted about me, I began to feel worse. Telling him you were heading out on vacation the next day, you suggested he take a final look at my gums before he left. You wanted to make sure I did not need to receive any fluids at his clinic. He lifted my upper life and told you my gums had turned gray, a clear sign I was colicking.

Sure enough, my condition was now deteriorating, and you were told to trailer me to his hospital for further testing and IV treatments.

My status went downhill quickly. Pretty soon, I could not stand up. Heavily sedated, I was still in excruciating pain. Struggling to hold my own, it was clear something was seriously wrong.

Given my age, surgery was out of the question. It was evident I could not be saved so you made a quick decision to help me transition. It was the right move, one you would not regret. My health history over the past year suggested I was ready.

From the morning to early afternoon, my body began to shut down. Although you realized it was my time to leave, making the final decision to euthanize me was a tremendous shock. You had not expected how swiftly my vitality would spiral, clearly indicating there was no other solution than euthanasia.

Fortunately, there was a crystal store a mile away. You had time to head there, returning with an amethyst shaped heart. As the vet helped me cross to the Spirit world, you held the beautiful stone on my forehead, at my third eye. I took my last breath with you by my side while the amethyst heart captured my soul essence. I made a swift exit to the Spirit realm.

While my soul transited to the other side, its imprint was enshrined in the amethyst crystal, preserving my memory forever.

My Past Lives

I have had many interesting past lives. Some of the most memorable are highlighted here. My lifetime with you was truly the most audacious. I was chosen to coach your own spiritual path, a great honor for a horse.

During the First Crusade of the 11th century, I was the highest commander Godfrey of Bouillon's warhorse, gallantly carrying him into many battles. Godfrey, with his brothers Eustace and Baldwin, joined the First Crusade in 1096. When Raymond of Toulouse declined to become king of Jerusalem, Godfrey accepted the crown but refused the title of king and was called instead Advocatus Sancti Sepulchri (Defender of the Holy Sepulcher).

We survived the war, and our lives continued together until his death in the year 1100. This was a very brutal lifetime, where I witnessed many horses and humans suffer enormously for the conquest of land and power. Thankfully this was the only lifetime where I saw destruction, war, and unnecessary death on a large scale.

After that lifetime, I chose to come back as an Irish farm horse. While most were trained to drive carts or work harrows in the field, I carried my master all over the country to visit his wards and collect rent from his landowners. It was a cherished time with benevolent owners and a casual lifestyle.

I was a Friesian stallion at a big Dutch farm in the 1800s. My noble breeding required ultimate care with groomers, handlers, and fine forage. The breeding barn was enormous, and I regaled in mating with many beautiful mares. We were reputed for producing magnificent foals over the course of many generations. Our offspring were exported to Germany and other countries to keep the Friesian bloodlines alive. Many of today's Friesian ancestors were of my lineage.

I was also an English carriage horse in the 1900s, working for a wealthy family who lived out in the country. I carried their family and friends around for two decades. Also well taken care of, I never suffered at the hands of malnourishment, or abuse.

The last lifetime before I met you was spent as a racehorse. I was quite fast, but not fast enough to become a winner. I was retired at the age of ten to become a stud horse in Kentucky. I happily spent the next ten years there, living on pasture and mating with many mares.

During these varied life experiences, my preferred soul agreements evolved into the profound bliss found between horse and human.

My Teaching: Impermanence Revealed in a Dream

The moment we met in a dream state, you knew my essence had traveled safely across the veil. Large as life, I was staring directly into your eyes, my penetrating gaze offering an important message. I was telling you I was free, a formless, pure Spirit.

You understood your dream was not an illusion but a Divine truth. While some might question whether my appearance in the dream plane was real, my presence was so tangible it left no shadow of a doubt in your mind.

In an instant, the power of impermanence was revealed to you.

When you woke up, you exclaimed, "I know you are pain free, Billy. You came to me in a dream, proving you still exist on a soul level. You brought clarity and peace to my grieving." Even though you could no longer touch or see my physical body, my appearance brought you enormous comfort.

Spirit made contact on the soul level, proving unequivocally life exists after death, nourishing us with an alternate reality.

For heart-centered soul-soul contracts, we visit after we depart our bodies. While it is not a difficult process, we will wait for the right timing once we have processed our physical death. Allow us the space to settle quietly in the Spirit realm and renew our momentum before we orchestrate a visit to you. Sometimes this may take time if we have endured great suffering or a prolonged illness before we die.

Here are the steps of the process. First, a belief in the unseen power of the soul is critical. A faithful gesture sets you up for the ensuing interactions. Trust the real power of soul-soul interactions.

Second, have confidence we will show up for you in any number of ways. You may meet up with one of us who has crossed to the Spirit world while dreaming, meditating, praying, or performing a shamanic journey. You may feel our presence when you touch an object which belonged to us, carrying our energy. Another person or animal may bring a message for you.

When you are paying attention to the signs, the visitations will be evidential.

We always respond, so be aware and ready for our signs. You may feel tingles up and down your spine when you import us into your thoughts. Another form of Divine truth, your angels and guides will appear, confirming your intuition is correct. All of these are indications of the soul's impermanence and its ability to project into present time.

These types of meetups occur on an unseen vibrational level. Know unconditionally we are with you or sending messages. The clues are unmistakable, confirming our palpable presence.

Tapping into this eternal source of information, there are many ways we can be together in the Spirit realm even if one of us is no longer in a body.

Life goes on, manifested by the impermanence of the soul.

Chapter 8

I Am Monty, an Appendix

I am a crossbreed between a Quarter horse and a Thoroughbred. Known as an Appendix, this intentional mix combines the speed and endurance of a Thoroughbred racehorse and the calm, sturdy temperament of a Quarter horse. Many Appendix horses are tall and lanky like the Thoroughbreds, and yet have a very strong muscular-skeletal makeup like a Quarter horse.

I was born on a small farm in North Dakota. My humans didn't qualify as breeders, so they were experimenting with this mix and match approach. Their goal was to produce winning racehorses, and they didn't care how they reached their quota.

The farm was run-down and filthy. The mares were used in back-back breeding programs, producing foals way too frequently for their own health. Therefore, they were unhealthy, and exhausted.

With no concern for the horses' well-being, the whole operation was inhuman and cruel.

My first memories were with my mamma. She barely had enough milk to nurse me. With little initial colostrum, I was underweight and malnourished. Nonetheless, she tried her hardest to love and nurture me.

I was weaned too early, creating severe separation anxiety and fear in my young life. Grouped with all the other colts and fillies, it was a lackluster and depressing time for all of us. A gloomy future awaited most of the herd as we were immediately shipped off to new destinations.

I found myself at another farm with a smaller number of horses. It was clear this was a racehorse training facility given the tracks, cooling racks and staff. I began to wonder what was coming next.

My training started the following year when I was two. Intense and harsh, this did not suit me at all. I did not appreciate the whips, chains, and constant jerking on my mouth.

I began to distrust all humans, especially those who abused and hurt my body.

My Trauma

Following the degrading ways I was treated as a youngster, I was raced as a three-year-old. Just the thought of running my fastest around a large track was enough to make me dizzy. Resistant to the training methods, I was whipped and beaten to make me do what they asked. Instead of encouraging me to move forward, I tried to buck and escape, which made things worse.

Eventually I gave in, allowing the trainers to put me through the paces. The starting gate was the first obstacle. Because I was hesitant, they placed a horse at my tail to make sure I left the gate with a big start. This felt unnatural, and I was not happy. But this was only one small part of the problem.

Once the horses left the gate, we were running for our lives. The footing was often slippery, making it difficult to gain traction and stay balanced. Most jockeys carried a whip, which they used freely to urge us on. This was painful and harsh, especially for a sensitive fellow like me.

I did not like the feeling of being neck to neck with other horses, crashing into their sides while we lost our minds in a speed race. It was dangerous because our back feet could be clipped from a horse coming up behind us, causing an accident, or worse. We were so close we could hear them panting and grunting, which increased my anxiety.

One race was especially traumatic. A very young jockey was riding me. Chosen for his confident attitude, his inexperience was clear as he shoved me into the starting gate. As we blasted out, he was very wobbly on my back, making it hard for me to steady my pace.

His uneven weight in the stirrups threw my balance off, and I fell hard on the track. He landed hard on the dirt, shattering the bones in his arm. His pain revealed the sorrow I felt in my heart, a devastating moment for me.

Racing was not for me. Seeing a young person so injured was difficult enough. Continuing racing was an impossible request for me.

I, too, was hurt. My back ached, and I longed to be retired from the sport.

At this point, my spirit was broken to the point of checking out. My trainer noticed my lackluster attitude. Given my lack of will to continue, my owner agreed to pull me from the track.

I was put up for auction again, one of the luckiest days of my life.

Racing Is Not for the Faint of Heart

For some horses, the racing world is a heartless and painful experience. You may enjoy watching this rough and competitive sport, but many of us are not suited for its arduous and rigorous techniques. Racing is not for the faint of heart.

Of course, we love to run. Our conformation is built for endurance and speed. Combined with our desire to please you, many of us do not confront you, agreeing to do something we are simply uncomfortable with.

The racing industry's parameters are physically, emotionally, and mentally difficult. You start us as youngsters, before our bones are fully formed and strong. The training demands are huge, asking us to work with different trainers and conditions.

We are also asked to trust those who care for our bodies to know when we are fatigued, hungry and sore. It often does not line up on our end, when we feel depleted and taken advantage of. On racing day, we are challenged to perform feats of swiftness, agility, and speed.

Crowding us into racing gates feeds into our deepest fight or flight instincts. Those of us who "succeed" in your eyes are champions; those who fail are given up for neglect, abuse, and slaughter. If we resist the training routines, we might also face the whips, nose chains and drugs.

We may never recover from our racing experiences.

Some of us give it all to our humans, demonstrating the courage and tenacity to become true champions. Others who go the distance fade into unknown statistics. For those of us who do not make the grade of "racehorse," we ask you to make early decisions to find another profession for us rather than put us through the motions of something which does not align with our highest good.

Our Meetup

My equine guides had told me a female human was coming into my life. They reassured me her arrival would be Divinely timed. I anticipated this moment, hoping I would recognize her. I had no idea just how synchronous our meetup would be.

I was down and out at the end of my racing career. Feeling l like a failure, the next stop was my new stint as a dude string horse. My nerves were jittery as they unloaded the large group from the stock trailers into the enormous holding area. How could I be expected to carry inexperienced riders on my back when the last job I had was all about galloping blindly down a racetrack?

A lot of activity was buzzing all around me when I arrived at the dude ranch. A couple dozen horses were tied up, eyeing one another. Some established rank while others were curious about their new herd mates. The farrier was shoeing many of them, while the veterinarian checked for soundness, and signs of illness or stress.

Meeting you was the farthest thing from my conscious mind. I had all I could do to hold my ground amidst new friends and an unfamiliar environment. I whinnied loudly, hoping to recognize a familiar face among the horses who arrived at the same time as I.

The last thing I expected was meeting you. You appeared out of the blue, entering the arena as silently as a mouse. There you stood, watching the activities like an animated movie.

When I saw you, I knew you were the one.

I observed the wonderment and eagerness in your eyes. Clearly you were drawn to me by my enormous whinny. Shiny and strong, my bold personality was also calling you.

I, too, wondered about the lady who stepped right into my energy field and openly presented herself as an inquisitive Spirit. I had piqued your curiosity. You had no idea our paths had crossed for a reason.

Spirit guided you directly into my life.

You quickly learned I was only three years old when I arrived at the ranch. While I was a tall and handsome fellow, I was still quite young and inexperienced. My short-lived career on the racetrack left me feeling vulnerable and unsure about what was expected of me.

I did not yet understand trail horses are expected to be calm, carrying all levels of riders on their backs. I was nervous and unsettled in my new surroundings, learning what my job would entail. It was my first season at a public dude ranch, and I knew they were undecided about whether to let me carry guests since I was quite jumpy and spooky.

Finding my way as a trail horse was going to be tricky. It was possible that my uneasy behavior would curtail my usefulness as a dude string horse. The wranglers then shared a very important piece of information with you. They said I was going to "auction" the following winter unless I carried my weight as a dude ranch horse.

I knew horses who went to the auction never came home.

I recognized your energy, knowing it was something we had shared in previous lifetimes. Filled with loving kindness, your heart was open and willing to embrace new beginnings. I could sense this light was expanding, reaching into my own field.

While we really didn't interact much, I heard the questions you were asking. Realizing our energy fields were already entangled, the alignment was happening.

Now it was a question of timing.

Given you understood I might be heading for the auction the following winter, I was hopeful you would come back to get me sooner than later. When you did arrive the following January, I was in poor shape. Hungry and tired, my weight had dropped significantly, and my emotional state was a wreck.

You acted swiftly, offering a nice sum of money to buy me. My owner agreed, and the two of you arranged a drop-off location where I would be transferred into your trailer to go home with you. Despite the fear inside me, it was a momentous day in my life.

Arriving at your home was peaceful. The other two horses greeted me in a most friendly manner, so I felt welcomed. Food and water were plentiful. I even had my own stall, so no one could steal my food or bully my space.

I was safe.

Our Spirit guides convened to arrange the meetup circumstances. You were instructed to take me home and help me heal. Even though you did not yet understand the significance of our odyssey, I was chosen as the second horse to carry forth the Triune's mission.

It was the beginning of a lifelong change for both of us.

Peppermints

The first year of my life with you was all about food. Plenty of hay was provided. You worked sensitively around me, touching me when possible, and always talking to me. Could I trust another human being?

In a state of complete starvation, it was unclear whether I would heal from the neglect and abuse that shaped my early life.

I gained weight as I began to feel secure. My long and slow recovery enabled us to forge a soul-soul bond. The seeds of Divine truth were disclosed as I progressed in my healing journey, inspiring you to seek more answers.

When you found the tattoo on the inside of my upper lip, you understood the significance of my racing history. The tattoo explained much of my erratic behavior. My jumpiness was unsettling to everyone who tried to handle me, especially you.

Trimming my hooves was a tricky, complicated process. I danced around, avoiding the farrier's attempts to hold up my feet. Given my strong flight instincts, I wanted to run away.

To make the training process easier, you used peppermints as motivational treats. Boy did I respond to those!

The minute I held up a foot long enough for the rasp, you said, "Good boy!" That praise was immediately followed by a peppermint. I quickly learned "good boy" meant I was going to get a treat.

I learned to be patient waiting for those treats. They came predictably with my trim sessions. My focus became the candy instead of moving my foot away from the stand. There was a direct correlation between the peppermints and my tolerance level.

My fear turned into pride as I slowly gained the trust of the people working with me. I made choices about how to behave and what awaited me when I did what was asked. A swift learner, I enjoyed the process.

My true, outgoing personality began to emerge.

Like Billy, I had a huge sense of humor. I became more charismatic as my comfort level increased in my new home. When I shifted from fear to love, my whole temperament changed. A new energy unfolded, confirming my curious and outgoing self.

Thanks to peppermints and lots of love, life was worth living.

My Job as Your Protector

I was like your big brother. It seemed very natural to me since our partnership was one of give and take. You felt I was your shield, offering emotional and physical protection.

When we rode, your worldly cares melted. You were yourself, with no one supervising or trying to influence your thoughts. I was happy to take the lead.

I was confident and strong, just like a caring big brother.

I reminded you to be present and mindful while riding the trails. A tranquility like nothing else you had experienced, we both were completely attuned to the mountains, sky, and clouds. The silence was deepening.

My protective role was the start of our ongoing communications. Because you were in a receptive state of consciousness, you were open to hear the messages I transmitted. When you asked my opinion, I gave it truthfully. A high level of psychic exchange was critical in our ongoing relationship.

The Trailer

For some of us, the trailer means prison. Unable to move or get out, it becomes a claustrophobic situation like the starting gate. We might be able to stay calm when we are buddied up inside.

Sometimes a terrifying experience, trailer loading can produce a panic attack.

It may be traced back to racing when we are stuck in the starting box, a tight and pressured space. With nowhere to go except forward, the box causes anxiety. Those who resist the gate are "tailed," a technique where our tail is held straight up in the air, causing great discomfort. When we feel the excruciating pain, we are forced to hold still and move forward when the starting gate flies open.

Traumatized, my noncompetitive personality was a misfit for the racing profession. When they locked the starting gate, I felt cornered. I was unable to move or leave on my own.

Humiliated, I was forced to run the race.

I resisted loading, especially when I felt pressure coming from you. Feeling your frustration, I became more fearful. When you resorted to more pressure, it went downhill because I refused to stay inside.

It was an unfortunate combination, but I was again your teacher. I made it clear what was working, and what was not. A trainer told you to tie me to the front of the trailer. You knew this would not work but allowed her to try anyway.

After a near accident using her method, you fired her.

We had many restarts, making countless mistakes along the way. You blamed yourself each time I demonstrated my unwillingness to stay put in the trailer long enough to close the bar. You eventually learned to trust yourself, understanding the slow and quiet way worked every time. This type of whispering eventually translated into everything else we did together.

And boy did you learn.

Many years later you realized standing there and pointing one finger in the trailer would load me up calmly. Your words were just as important: "Take your time." And you had to mean it—everything a word of it. If you were rushing or frustrated, I shut down.

I trained you to be calm and put your anxiety aside. When I felt your nervousness, I became uneasy and jumpy. The slightest amount of frustration in our connection ended the training session. You learned to be very patient, asking me to get into the trailer in a soft and gentle way without insisting with a whip or pressure.

I complied when you gave me permission to exit, quietly waiting for my agitated behavior to settle down.

I could back out quietly, without blasting my way backwards. How dangerous was I? I'm sorry I put you through those experiences, but your mistakes made you a better horse whisperer and companion.

Imagine how Romeo would be now if you had pressured him into submission. How controlling.

I was your supreme instructor. Understanding your commitment to learning and evolving, I molded some of your behavior based on my reactions and emotions. I did a good job because you changed.

You developed the skills of mindfulness and patience.

Passing the Spiritual Baton to Romeo

I was sick. I could feel the pain in my mid-belly, radiating down my spine to my tail. The saddle was uncomfortable on my back. It wasn't a sharp pain, but a dull ache, pressing under the saddle.

The summer it started, I would jerk my head sideways. An unusual motion for me, you knew something had changed. It was intense for you because my reactions were so strong and sudden. You sensed something big was happening; I was starting my journey to the Spirit realm.

To prepare for my eventual crossing, I decided to convene with Romeo. I talked to him about our roles with humans. He was devoted to me, his master. Yet, his idea of being with a human was very different than mine, and I had 18 years with you to share my experiences.

Romeo was used to being pushed around by wranglers. He was conditioned to behave without thinking. Shut down emotionally, I knew he buried his feelings deep inside. A good observer, Romeo was ready process those feelings into his sensitive soul.

As his teacher, I could impart my experiences to him.

I told him to be with a human is to understand human emotions. I learned how to read you, a highly vibrational human. I was high-strung enough on my own, let alone in partnership with you.

Over the years, I used my breath to help you slow down, pay attention, and be more present and mindful around me. You and I learned from listening to each other. By the end of my life, we perceived every emotional interchange, mood and feeling. This is what I shared with him.

It was Romeo's turn to be with a sensitive, caring human. I told him to stay very grounded, be aware of what he was experiencing and take good care of you. He took my advice.

I explained you rely on us for protection and comfort. I demonstrated how my silent leadership could be replicated without violence and aggression, even when I was afraid. I showed him ways to interact with you which would establish confidence in your budding relationship.

I also told Romeo humans do make mistakes, to forgive yours when they occur.

Romeo is a very ascended soul. He witnessed the suffering equines have borne. He would take over my job, stepping into my place as your main horse. Not as a protector, but a very deep soul mate for you, and the loving relationship you have built together.

The two of you have your own special soul agreement. His unconditional love shines forth, embellishing the devotion you share together. At the end of my days, I felt the peace in my heart knowing a strong bond was forming between you.

I had complete faith Romeo would step into my big shoes, filling them completely.

My Time to Leave

Something inside me was changing. The pain in my belly moved from my rib cage to the base of my spine. I took it all in stride, understanding the life cycle. I also knew telling you would create tremendous worry and stress. My life could not be saved, so I concealed my pain, acting like nothing was wrong.

One day I could no longer hide my condition. I was in such agony, I could not eat, nor drink. You understood my status when you fed me breakfast. Concerned, you gave me homeopathic remedies for colic, performing energetic techniques to mitigate my symptoms. You scanned my eyes.

They, too, revealed the seriousness of my illness.

Later in the day you phoned the vet, who came to our barn. She took my temperature and drew blood. She told you she would have the results later in the day. The situation was terminal, but I couldn't let you know quite yet.

The vet thought I had an infection because my white blood count was elevated. Feeling quite poorly, I still had no appetite or thirst. I was sure my body was done; now it was opportune to let you know what was going on.

When you came out at 4 a.m. the next morning, I saluted you with my loud whinny. For a split second, you looked relieved. But my greeting was not a sign of recovery.

I was sending you a clear heart-to-heart message: my transition was imminent, and my soul was content and happy with this closure.

The shock set in when you saw how much I was bleeding. My tail and back end were covered in blood. Realizing the severity of the situation, the look on your face said it all. Now you had to process how the day was going to play out. You tried very hard to be brave, but I knew this was going to be a very difficult time for you.

You quickly loaded Romeo and me into the trailer and hauled us to the vet's office so they could check me one last time. It was a long ride, and I complied well with loading. After an exam, the vet told you there was nothing more they could do for me. The appointment was made for later that day to help me cross to the Spirit world.

With a heavy heart, you asked me to get back into the trailer, telling me you wanted to bury me at home rather than put me down at the vet's office. Given our difficult loading history, I obliged. I wasn't about to cause a fuss at the vet and let you say your final goodbyes there.

I gave you one last gift when I climbed back into the trailer. Your gratitude was immense.

You chose a burial spot overlooking the gorgeous BLM land where we had ridden. With the family surrounding me, we gathered facing the mountains. When the vet arrived, the ceremony was ready.

I felt your immense love and devotion. I knew my angels were around me, waiting to escort me home.

Swiftly and cleanly, a hasty departure was the only way for me to leave you. I did not suffer long. Only the last few hours were challenging for me. When you saw the hives all over my body, you knew I was shutting down quickly. My body was guiding the process, releasing my soul to the afterlife.

An overwhelming sense of peace came over me as my body shut down. Your help that day was a gift, expediting my transit to heaven. Given my failing condition, the euthanasia went as smoothly as possible.

My soul departure was clean and swift.

It was so hard for you to say goodbye to me. Our time together on Earth lasted 20 long and glorious years. I knew my sudden death left a huge void in your life, both physically and spiritually. I passed all the lessons along to you during our journey together. We moved through abandonment, fear, safety, trust, bliss, patience and many more issues.

I appointed my death when it was time for you to work on your multidimensional self. You had reached a level of spiritual development, but my presence was holding you back. Recognizing our psychic connection, you acknowledged me as your protector and your shield.

You questioned me repeatedly, asking why I had to leave so suddenly. Had I revealed how sick I was, you would have tried everything in your power to heal me. You would have made yourself crazy seeking solutions, none of which would have prolonged my life.

My sudden death was not a breach of contract but a wake-up call to face your fears, step into your power and reach for Divine guidance.

My Past Lives

You knew the moment our eyes met we had been together before. There was a familiarity about me you could not identify. An intuitive feeling told you we were old friends.

Since our meetup occurred long before you began your formal psychic training, it did not occur to you that we shared previous lifetimes together. Your consciousness was not wide enough to grasp that concept.

After several years, you perceived our multi-life contracts. You began investigating why my departure had such a serious and devastating impact upon your soul. Your confusion and bewilderment created an enormous learning opportunity for you, guiding you to study the impact of past lives in one's current situation.

Our lifetimes together date back hundreds of years. You discovered we shared nine previous lifetimes, each one with a different mission and relationship. Our experiences varied; some were smooth while others were quite difficult.

> *One lifetime built upon the previous one, ramping up the relationship until it reached a healing peak.*

In one lifetime, I was a farm horse in Ireland. Short and stocky, I was reliable and steady. I carried you to school around the countryside. We shared long, playful adventures. I lived 27 years, a healthy and strong lifetime.

We served in several wars together. I took you into battle many times in the Middle Ages, the European wars between the 1400s–1500s, and most recently, the Spanish-American War. Each time, I guarded and protected you, valiantly putting my life before yours.

Several other lifetimes were spent in conflict situations during the wars in Europe and the British Isles. I was a warhorse, serving as your guardian and protector. We fought valiantly together, surviving these tragic times together.

Yes, you were a male human in those days, but it need not matter.

Fear was a recurrent theme during the warzones as horse-human partners. Enduring bloodshed and trauma put both of us under tremendous strain. The bond between us was unbreakable, especially due to my role as your defender.

Prior to our reconnection this time around, I spent one lifetime as a standard bred trotting horse. A champion, I was a swift, chestnut fellow who was started as a two-year-old. I was good at my job, pulling the one-man cart around the track. It would not have been my choice; although I liked to run, I did not enjoy having a contraption strapped to my body.

I raced for seven years, winning many events. Eventually I was retired to a stud farm in Ohio where I lived out the rest of my days peacefully. The career chosen for me wore out my body, but at least the humans were gracious enough to respect my post racing days and allow me to be a horse living in the open fields of a big breeding farm.

There is no doubt you felt my protective shield during each iteration, including this lifetime. When I died at age 23 this time around, you found yourself in a complete vacuum. My death created a temporary void, even the memories or grateful thoughts around our multi-lifetime partnership did not soothe your soul in the beginning.

The emptiness was enormous, causing tremendous conflict and confusion in your space. Completely immobilized by sadness, your energy was stuck. Your inability to move forward after my death was a palpable force to reckon with us during this lifetime. We had a great deal of clearing to accomplish, individually and collectively.

The energetic programs were repeating themselves; it was time to release the lingering fears of abandonment in your soul. With this lifetime's closure, you finally received enough past life information to help process any outliers in our extended history together. We cleared a lot of fear in this lifetime, creating the space for enormous healing.

Removing myself from our co-creative relationship propelled you into a completely new phase of your life. Holding yourself accountable, you now must walk an authentic path. New opportunities for spiritual development are available, revealing your mission on Earth.

The present moment holds great promise for spiritual expansion.

We are still so connected, having been together in nine past lives. When you want to speak to me, ask. I will provide advice and comfort. Even though you cannot see me, I am here. I have brought many messages to you from the other side.

I continue to watch over you every day. Our unified soul path continues, outlasting my lifetime.

My Teaching: Pure Unconditional Love

When I arrived at your barn, my physical condition was dire. Close to starvation, I was a complete skeleton. My ribs protruded so much you were told to call a veterinarian and report my status to the state authorities.

In a precarious form, you did not know whether I would live or die.

After one full year of healing, we began the retraining process. There were innumerable mistakes and misunderstandings. Saddling, bridling, and even leading me off the property were frustrating at best.

Often, we both gave up when the pressure became too much to handle. You truly didn't know how to reach me emotionally. Instead, you talked to me constantly, telling me how much you loved me.

I could feel how hard you were trying. I understood you wanted to help me heal. Your love was unconditional, free from any expectations of whether I would ever be a reliable riding partner.

I began to trust after feeling the unconditional love bestowed upon me.

Chapter 9

I Am Romeo, a Mustang

I am an American mustang of Spanish descent. Born in 1998 in Susanville, California, our herd was quite large, with about 1000 horses living free on the open range. Like most Spanish mustangs, you can identify my lineage from my beautiful, curved nose. I have a strong conformation, with strong bones and a robust body.

Mustangs are a noble and proud breed. Distinct from other horses, we are cut from a different cloth. Because we are born on the open plains, our instincts are much more developed. From the moment our feet land on the ground, our physical senses are on high alert. Our first touch is by our mothers, then our herd members, then nature.

We migrate frequently to find food and water. Our awareness is tuned into the movements and noise in our surroundings. We think independently and fend for ourselves. Alert and resilient, we are tenacious and do not give up easily.

We live in an ordered fashion. There is a hierarchy among us, following certain guidelines about how to behave. We are wary of humans, who chase, terrify, and capture us to reduce our population.

Humans have broken our spirit repeatedly; many want to reduce our numbers and lock us away the rest of our lives.

Those of you who partner with us understand our sensitivity; this is who we are. It is not something you can train out of us. Once you learn and accept this, it will grace our friendships and partnerships with an easier flow.

This deep level of acknowledgement enables us to be ourselves and step into who we are, an ancient breed which has survived for centuries. We are extremely loyal and would die for our person. We've fought in wars, leading our humans into battle with fearlessness and confidence.

Being in our presence raises your human perceptiveness to a new level of awareness. We honor those of you who seek us out, showing you our devotion and loyalty. You become our person, our everything.

Our world revolves around you. You feel and know this on a very profound level. It's a human-equine love affair when it works. Once we've bonded with you, it is as if you are part of our herd. We will often perish if our beloved human dies or gives up on us.

Our bonding is for life, just as we do in the wild.

Growing Up in the Herd

I was born in an open field surrounded by other mothers and their foals. There were four stallions and twelve mares in my herd. My grandfather and father supervised where we roamed, when the mares were bred, and how the young were raised. We were nurtured and well cared for.

Being a productive young stallion, my father sired quite a few foals the year I was conceived. He was the quiet chief of the herd due to a commanding presence all the horses respected. A protector for his mares, the other stallions rarely challenged him. As our leader, he served as a great example of mustang strength and power. He was swift and fierce, an expert at smelling danger.

I had lots of half-brothers and sisters. Many of them would stay and become permanent members of the herd. The young stallions would eventually leave and form their own herds. If they left soon enough there would not be competition. Our range constituted thousands of acres, so there was enough land for all of us to coexist.

Life was peaceful and blissful. I had lots of playmates. With plenty of food and water, we had few concerns. Occasionally we heard about resident lions, but they rarely took one of us for food because we were so strongly bonded. We were a carefree herd.

Because our herd was growing fast, the government decided our numbers needed to be culled, using traditional capture methods like helicopters and trucks to gather us into holding pens. From there, we were transported to numerous locations across the country. This was, and continues to be, a cruel and heartless means of population control.

I was captured when I was two years old, old enough to run about on my own away from my mates. I was growing well, confident as could be for a young stallion. Once in captivity, the deep emotional wounds left me spiritless and uninterested in the world around me.

The shock of my capture left an indelible impression on me, one that took years to unwind.

Family

Like you, our families are very important to us. It begins with our mothers, who give us life and nourish our every need. Our elders teach us early lessons around herd bonding, safety, and cooperation. We were reprimanded if we got out of line or broke the rules. Mustang herds have a hierarchy.

Guided wisdom and experience, we observe and learn from our family members.

Our stallions are just as important as our mares. They safeguard the herds, and the individual mares who are part of their harem.

At birth, they protect the babies from predators and other stallions who might want to hurt us.

Herd dynamics within our families are critical for survival of the fittest. The young cannot fend for themselves, so they rely upon older siblings, parents, and grandparents to educate them as wild horses. Any foal born in a weakened state is likely to die unless its family watches out for its welfare. This means others will help find food, water and resting places when roaming about the open plains and mountains.

When our families are divided, we all suffer. It doesn't matter who is captured, taken away or separated from our core herds. It is a destructive means to control our breeding and growth. The ensuing trauma from these schisms lasts for decades as the herd members grieve, attempting to rebuild their families. Removing the young and old in our herds shatters our tribes.

Life changes in a matter of hours for many wild horses. One moment we are moving quietly along the grand, vast, million-acre spaces we call home. The next moment, we are rounded up and taken away from our beloved families, wreaking havoc on the captured and the remaining horses.

The heartbreak is deep and long lasting.

Humans need to be aware this is not the natural order. Culling our herds via capture is a cruel force, destroying our family structures, bonds, and survival. We, the American mustangs, continue to ask for protection and humane means to keep our populations in check.

The Capture

We were on top of the ridge, our home and observation area. The helicopters were approaching, like huge monsters in the sky. Frightened, we began to run down into the valley. Suddenly the helicopters were all around us, surrounding us with a terrifying noise. Trucks circled the herd, advancing closer and closer. Men on horseback joined the chase.

A bad dream was unfolding right in front of our eyes.

The dust was swirling like a cyclone. There was tremendous fear for our herd safety. We were scattering, running into each other screaming. As we tried to escape, we were separated from our loved ones.

My father tried to lead us away from the danger. He ran hard and far, taking some of our herd members with him. He escaped but the rest of us were trapped. Over 100 horses, we finally froze in a bundle, all tightly huddled together. Traumatized and injured, many were falling. We could not see our family members but heard them calling.

After the helicopters rounded us up into large holding pens, the trucks started their job. They began to move us one by one, maneuvering us onto the transports. Some of the handlers tried to be gentle, knowing we were exhausted, terrified and thirsty.

The next step was just as brutal as the first.

My world collapsed as I was ushered onto a large stock trailer. Twenty of us crowded into the space. We dared not kick or bite each other even though our emotions were exploding with rage and anger at the humiliating treatment we had just witnessed.

It was the worst day of my life as I saw my mother, half-sisters and brothers loaded into other trucks.

One of my brothers was in the same truck as I, but he was completely unrecognizable. I saw my half-sister fall, then struggle to stand up. Badly injured, her front leg was bleeding. As the shocked horses were herded together, she fell behind, trying to regain her balance. As they stampeded toward the exit gate where the wranglers were pushing them, she fell again. I watched as she struggled to survive the roundup.

Prodded into a different large stock trailer, she disappeared into the dust as we remaining horses waited for our truck to leave. This time she didn't get up. Crushed beneath the thundering hooves, my dear herd mate perished. Covered with dust, the last thing I saw were her beautiful, kind eyes.

So began my time in captivity, where I began to understand the meaning of surrender.

Prison Life

After the capture, our group of horses was transported to the Wild Horse Inmate Program in Cañon City, Colorado. One of the largest wild mustang and burro operations in the country, as many as 3000 mustangs may be housed there at any given time. Horses from across the western states arrived; some were adopted out through their programs while others spent the rest of their lives living in large holding pens.

I buried my deep sadness inside for many years, not knowing if my life would ever change. I was given a job as a trainer's horse. My solid confirmation and willing attitude helped me stand out from the others.

As afraid as I was, I quickly figured out life would be better if I complied.

My human partner was a trainer, helping orient the young mustangs to their new routine. A kind man, he didn't relate to the horses emotionally. Although we did not bond, a cordial, working relationship was forged.

My duties were straightforward. I ponied green horses around the property, helping them get used to a halter and saddle. Eventually, I led them around the obstacle courses, showing them how to step up on ramps, cross over water and stand still when asked.

I grew accustomed to my new life in about six months. There were friends to be made and stories to be told since we shared our common ground—capture. I made some good buddies at the Cañon City prison. I witnessed horses come and go; many of them went to loving homes.

Knowing there was hope comforted those of us who were left behind.

I heard the talk around the prison. Some of the older mustangs were being taken to an unknown destination. They were planning on shipping us in large stock trailers to remote locations in Oklahoma or Kansas, depositing us there to live out the rest of our lives in holding pens. Or perhaps a worse fate.

There was simply no room at the Cañon City facility for us. Our living quarters were crowded, with more than ten mustangs living in twenty-foot square corrals. Tired and hungry, the squabbling among us was increasing.

The roundups had increased, so they needed to make room for the incoming, untrained mustangs.

This was a worrisome feeling. Many of us knew this was the end of the line. Living out our lives in outdoor, uncovered corrals in the middle of nowhere was not a viable option. Realistically, adequate food and water supplies would be difficult for any government facilities to maintain.

No one wanted to adopt an older mustang who had lived his or her whole life in the prison. It was more fashionable and trendier to take a green one home with minimal training. The young ones were sought after and adopted swiftly.

For those of us who were considered past our prime, it was a dire predicament.

Our Meetup

I spent twelve years doing exactly what was asked of me. Then one day I heard my person was retiring. Unsure of my future, I waited patiently to find out. There was talk of sending me off again. An unsettling feeling because horses who went somewhere undetermined did not return.

From their perspective, I was considered an older horse even though I was only 14. My old herd mates lived well into their twenties, so I did not view myself as finished doing my job. But the prison authorities did.

Adoption days were about once monthly. Young and beautiful mustangs were picked first, finding new homes with special humans. Sometimes, they returned to the prison with stories of failure from their new people.

It was a confusing message for me because I was not the type to give up, so I could not fathom letting my human down.

A group of people had arrived for adoption day. The flashiest babies were being presented to them. Some had already reserved their horses online, so their decisions had been set prior to their arrival. Others wanted to check out the ones listed on the official prison website.

We knew the drill as the few lucky ones were loaded onto trailers and hauled to their new homes.

It was warm, so summer had arrived. I had not been used for a while, so I was standing around in my pen. One of the wranglers came to get me. Saddled and ready to go, I had no idea what was to come. Having spent most of my life at the facility, my expectations were low.

I soon realized you had come to the prison, and the wranglers were hoping you would take me home.

You had spent the entire day observing our routine at the prison. I knew you had asked many questions about the horses and burros. You were curious about the inmates, and how they interacted with us.

You had come to see a different mustang, a three-year-old. He was lame, so you were unable to ride him. When the wranglers asked if you were interested in adopting me, you inquired whether you could ride me.

Suddenly I was taken from the cow pen where I lived and saddled up. I didn't know what was happening, but I felt a spark of excitement. Despite my wariness, I trusted one of the wranglers whose big heart earned him the reputation among us for being gentle and kind.

Cody took me to the round pen, where you were waiting. You were eager to meet me; the look on your face told me you were a sincere and caring human. Might you take me home?

You hopped on my back and there was an exchange between you and Cody. I was a trainer's horse, he explained. Now my trainer was retiring, so there was no place for me to go. The silence in the air was deafening.

Cody told you my purchase price was $75.00.

You made a five-minute decision to adopt me. My heart was beating so fast it almost jumped out of my chest. I was leaving the prison. You were my new human partner, showing up at precisely the right time. I had no idea how lucky I was.

Since your home was within the delivery radius, the main office told you they'd haul me to you. I wasn't sure where I was going, but I knew it was going to be much better than Oklahoma or Kansas. The deal was sealed.

A massive energetic shift was taking place. My soul was euphoric. I knew instinctively my life was about to become full of joy and happiness.

You saved my life.

A Day of Unknowns

For many years, I watched horses and burros come and go from the prison. I could not imagine where they were headed. The young ones were traveling to a new home. The older, compromised ones never returned, hauled off in large stock trailers. Those vehicles did not smell good when they came back. Perhaps it was the smell of death lingering in the dusty trailer bed.

Now it was my turn. Having no idea what was to become of me, was I to escape an unknown future? I could sense something was happening, especially since my trainer was retiring and they had discussed my future. I remembered your visit, and how you agreed to adopt me.

Two weeks had passed. Was I leaving the prison? I didn't understand why I was still there. Other horses left on visitation day with their new owners. Why was I still hanging around? Had the decision to rehome me changed?

It was a day of unknowns.

It occurred to me I hadn't been called up for my daily routine. After breakfast, there was no saddling up. I usually ponied the young mustangs around the prison grounds, encouraging them to accept the saddle while helping them adjust to spooky obstacles. Such was my prison job, instructing the newbies in the art of becoming a domesticated horse.

It was as if Spirit suddenly took charge and charged up the activity. A large, red stock trailer was sitting next to the corrals. A man I didn't know came to the door of our cow pen, holding a halter and lead I didn't recognize.

He was gentle and soft. I understood his energy immediately, beckoning me to follow. Then he loaded me into the stock trailer all by myself. While excited, I still wasn't sure where he was taking me.

I was deeply hopeful I was going to a better place than the prison where I had lived for twelve years. Was I going to some remote location in the middle of nowhere where I would live out my days with other, older mustangs? Or was I destined for a real home, with caring humans and a new lifestyle? I longed for the latter.

There I stood all alone, scared, and isolated. I had never experienced a trip by myself in a horse trailer. I mustered up all my courage, hoping I was heading to a better place.

I surrendered to the unknown, again.

It was a long haul, but a smooth ride. Pretty soon I could feel the elevation and temperature change. This felt very different than the dry weather in Cañon City. I watched as the scenery changed, and the foothills became more evident.

When the wrangler unloaded me on a paved road, I was a bit surprised until I saw you standing there waiting for me. I looked around, realizing this was not a large holding facility with other horses. It was lush and green pasture.

My New Home

I could not believe my eyes. I had not seen such a gorgeous sight since my early childhood in California. There was an abundance of beautiful grass and flowers for grazing and rolling.

I was in horse heaven.

There was a real barn with three stalls situated right smack in the middle of the twelve-acre field. Each stall had its own corral, opening to the pasture. Two other horses watched as we descended the hill. They were my new friends.

Now understanding I had been transported to a small, private home barn, I was overjoyed. This was a dream come true for me. As hard as my previous twelve years had been, I was free.

I had almost forgotten what it felt like to graze. My feet melted on grass. Cool, moist air filled my lungs. Running with the other two horses, memories of my young life on the plains came flooding back.

My new stable mates seemed quite agreeable. The big guy, Montana, was very curious about me. I could feel his glance as he gave me the once-over. We sniffed noses over the fence, a nice icebreaker.

I knew instinctively he was the boss, but not an aggressive or bullying type.

Sky was a stocky, persnickety quarter horse mare. When you let us out to graze, the two of them chased me all around the property, making sure I knew I was the new kid on the block. Luckily, I jumped over the fence from one pasture into the other so they could not bite or kick me.

Eventually the three of us because fast friends. I had my very own stall, with food and water. It was completely different from life at the prison, and I was liberated. What did I do to deserve such a glorious new life?

I ended up with a human who understands me. Had I stayed at the prison, I don't know what would've happened. I believe my life would've ended at only twelve years old.

Who knew you would tell my story? I am a voice to be heard among the tens of thousands who have been silenced.

Forever in Your Heart

This was not a conscious idea on my part, but I know how it happened. When you changed my name to Romeo, it suited me. I felt the energy unfolding between us, accepting my new role as a different kind of horse. Mustang was my breed, but horse-human kinship became my mission.

With my new name, I stepped into the part of a loving fellow. I felt love in my heart. You reciprocated, binding us into a spiritual oneness transcending our physical existence. I didn't know it was possible to share this with a human.

The situation might have played out differently for me. I'll never know, because I will live out the rest of my days with my friends, happily serving the humans who deeply care about my welfare. Making sure I am fed, warm and loved, I will never be abandoned again.

Into your heart I came. Your gentle ways earned my trust. Believing in me helped grow my confidence. Even when we had miscommunications, you faithfully pursued, trusting me every step of the way.

I blossomed with your love, like a lotus plant whose petals gradually unfolded, revealing many layers underneath.

Our relationship grew slowly and softly, revealing how deep human-horse bonding can be. I can feel every muscle in your body when you are on my back. When you turn your head, I know which direction your eyes are looking.

I can sense your emotions. I can intuit your feelings before you do. Happiness makes me feel giddy. Sadness is confusing and dark to me because it's an emotion I do not recognize like you do.

I can read your mind, even before you know it. Your thoughts have already crossed the cosmos before they enter your consciousness. It's tremendously fun to gauge your reaction once you realize I already heard what you are thinking.

I am forever in your heart.

The Interim

I was waiting, watching Monty "be" with a human. My previous experiences at the prison had shaped my life so far, but that was shifting. After my capture, I was paired with a human who called himself a horse trainer, but there was no connection between us. I lived in a dual reality, a separation of mind and body from Source.

Life at the prison was a disconnect in my life.

In the beginning, I was a terrified two-year-old, torn away from my family and herd. Truly a lost soul, I eventually learned to feel safe, making a few friends at the prison and watching the "wild horse program" unfold. My person, the trainer, barely interacted with me except to push me around with ropes and a harsh voice. He did not greet me as a sentient being, nor inquire how I was doing.

Now it was different. The vibration was interactive, a more even exchange between horse and human. I was not tasked with any demands or expectations. How refreshing was my new life?

The interim between my arrival and my role as a riding companion was spacious. Since I was allowed to just "be," I spent my time observing the barn atmosphere, soaking in the fluid dynamic around us.

Watching Monty was an endearing experience. He was a gentleman, knowing how to train you to the equine way. He shared stories of his youthful traumas with me. Not dissimilar from mine, they also echoed fear and mistrust of humans.

And he was abused. He had the hole in his head to prove it. But he healed under your gentle loving care, and so do I.

Every day he is gone, I remember the lessons he patiently taught me, the ones I'm repeating with you. I understand your anxious vibrations, where you are worried or fretting. Knowing you as well as I do, I can redirect your emotions to stay grounded by holding my composure.

I've stepped up now as your main riding horse. We are co-creating a confidence-building partnership based on mutual respect. We are moving through new lessons daily, buoying each other through the comfort zones into new areas of training. As partners, you encourage me to be my best possible self.

The love and caring feelings are reciprocal. I demonstrate my love for you in gentle ways. Putting my muzzle on your shoulder, or next to your head. Breathing deeply on your cheek. Inviting you to stroke my nose and kiss my face. I'm happy you changed my name to Romeo since it fits me perfectly.

I hoped equine-human relationships could be this magical, but I never imagined it would happen to me in this lifetime. I am truly blessed.

My Turn

Monty became my instant hero. Tall and handsome, he had a quiet leadership I admired instantly. His essence was commanding; yet, he was not pushy or aggressive.

Monty knew everything. I watched in amazement how he asked for attention, begged for treats and behaved under saddle. How did he get to this level of interaction with you? I knew he had moved through his personal trauma to reach this point of trust with you, bringing new energy into your lives.

It was a seamless relationship. I could tell you read each other's minds. Monty was able to relay messages to you through his body language and his breath. It was fun and magical to observe.

I wanted to emulate this fellow equine. There were limitless opportunities to learn and imitate him, so I did. Monty, you, and I were all part of a small herd, cooperating and interacting with mutual respect. If he could heal in the presence of a loving, caring human, so could I.

I decided to send you this message: "I watch Monty interact with you, learning many things from him. I see he is a gentleman, treating you with respect and kindness. I see the two of you are patient with one another. I observe how humans and horses could interact without a lot of push and control issues."

I don't have to be afraid of how humans will treat me; you are fair, genuinely wishing to understand me. It is a huge gift from Monty to me, one I am forever grateful for. I want to step up now and be your partner. I don't mean to be spooky; I do feel the energetic vibrations you emit when you are unsure or nervous. I know you thought I didn't pick up on them, but the circumstances are different now and it's you and me in a partnership.

So, the communication channels need to be crystal clear. No doubt. Doubt will cloud our relationship and leave me confused. This is my message for you.

Shock

I was in a state of complete shock for many weeks following Monty's death. His sudden departure left an enormous void in our lives. His large physical presence had vanished, along with his amazing whinny and outgoing personality.

The silence around the barn was deafening. The impact of his death was palpable and heavy. You tried your hardest to find any shreds of joy, but you could not get past the emptiness for months. I, too, felt lost and abandoned.

He was a great friend to me. A leading example of equine leadership I had never known before and during my years at the prison. And for you, I knew he was like your big brother, offering protection and unconditional love.

The sense of despair permeated our riding partnership. Now I had stepped up into the lead horse position, a brand new feeling for me. As honored as I was, I was also unsure of my new role. I could feel the waves of sadness through your body down your legs and into my back.

I knew you were going through the motions, trying to find the happiness in the saddle when all you could think of was Monty. Some of your sadness translated directly into fear, because you understood I was still developing as your main riding horse.

My behavior could be unpredictable, spooking when I saw something move in the bushes or along the trail. This fear spiraled downward until we both felt it every time we went out on a ride. There was one incident which really dismantled your confidence when I bolted seeing hikers coming around a corner with their dogs and walking poles.

Sending me in a tailspin, I almost dumped you on the road.

An unfortunate episode, it spurred you into rethinking our relationship. It was like starting from scratch, learning the basics about one another. You discovered clicker training as a new form of positive reinforcement to help me develop confidence on the trails.

Clicker training was a game changer for us. We focused on cooperative solutions, embarking on a new phase of our relationship. The fear which was shutting down our connection was dispelled, moving into a space of unconditional love and discovery.

Relying on each other for strength and courage helped both of us heal the shock of an unforeseen tragedy. We were lost, searching for ways to forge a new, joyful connection. Even though Monty's sudden death left us both in a vacuum of grief, the eventual outcome was a period of tremendous healing.

Our co-creative partnership blossomed when fear was replaced with love.

My Past Lives

My most notable past life was spent as one of six stallions kept in the court of Spanish King Philip II in the mid-1500s. An avid horseman, King Philip founded the studbook for the Spanish horse at the Royal Stables in Cordoba. Although I was not one of the original breeding stock used to establish these prized European bloodlines, my background was Andalusian.

I served Philip II as one of his personal riding horses. With my gentle nature, I was a trusted and reliable companion horse for him. I was not used in warfare or cavalry; instead, I carried him in parades and royal events around the country.

It was a peaceful and loving lifetime. I lived a long life, fathering many young ones for the ultimate Spanish horses who were sold to Italy, France, England, and Germany. Many famous Andalusian bloodlines continue to flourish today because of our strong and beautiful ancestors from this era.

Another lifetime was spent with the Spanish conquistadors who came to the Americas in the later part of the 16th century. We came by boat; there were 40 horses with the soldiers. Known for my bravery and leadership, I was chosen to make the journey with 15 other males. The rest were female, who were used for breeding once we arrived on the shores of the Americas.

The explorers who brought our herd from Spain landed in Central America. From there, they traveled to Mexico, where they colonized the territories. Moving north, we carried soldiers, supplies and food.

It was a difficult lifetime as a soldier's horse. We were ridden for many hours, traveling over the mountains and deserts of the southwest as we moved north. I was one of the lucky ones who was cared for by the conquistador commanders; others perished from lack of food and water. Some were turned loose to find their own way of survival.

The mustang breed flourished in the wilderness for centuries before man began to catch us and keep us in captivity.

My next lifetime in the 1800s was spent on a cattle ranch in the southwestern United States. I was part of a working herd which originated from the sturdy Mexican conquistador horses. Strong and steady, I served my humans with loyalty and courage.

From then on, I chose to reincarnate as an untamed mustang horse. I was ready to thrive on the range. While it was challenging, I chose a life of open living, representing ultimate liberty for a horse.

It was a magnificent experience, one I hold dear in my soul.

A life of freedom ensued, up until this current lifetime where I was captured and sent off to a holding pen. From there, I landed in the Wild Horse Inmate Program at the Federal Prison in Cañon City, Colorado. The rest is history, illustrated here in this very book.

You are wondering if you and I shared a past life together? No, this is our first go around. Even though the newness of our relationship has long worn off, we continue to cover unexplored territory as our journey unfolds.

My Teaching: Love from the Heart

Heartfelt love is eternal, superseding time and space. Originating inside the heart chakra, this love radiates into your entire aura. This is a Divine essence, the deepest form we know.

The heart chakra is the greatest portal in the physical body to emit and receive love. Its centered radiance fills you up, creating a safe and secure shield. This chakra has the capacity to expand and contract with love's vibrations.

Horses love categorically from our hearts. Through this exchange, we feel your heart's vibrational output. Then we increase ours, amplifying the connecting pulsation. If you really want to know us, learn to feel the love we emanate through our hearts.

Once we have established this heart-heart relationship with you, we express love completely. We accept your mistakes forgivingly, understanding your humanness may get in the way of loving us as purely as we love you. Our unconditional love cannot be changed or broken.

Love consciously from your heart. Keep this channel open and clear. Feel how the love vibration brings blissful feelings and emotions. Occupy this space with pure thoughts and emotions, remaining available to give and take heartfelt love in all aspects of your life.

You will discover unbridled passion arising from our authentic, heart-centered love.

Part III

Spirit Manifests

Chapter 10

Signs from Beyond the Veil

There is an entire world beyond your physical reality. What you see, feel, hear, touch and smell is only one plane of existence. Unlimited information is available to you on this soul level. Your Spirit team bestows offerings, gifts, messages, and signs from beyond the veil.

Nature herself is a conveyor of messages. A bird flying across your path is a sign. A cloud formation resembling your favorite dog in Spirit is a clue to his presence in the afterlife. A feather lying on the ground under your feet contains your special message.

Feathers are love notes from the messengers, the birds. Birds can send and receive information from both the earthly and Spirit planes, so they offer a bridge between those two worlds. Birds also carry the wind on their backs, so their energy fields are receptors for the unseen, subtle tidings residing in the Earth's etheric layers.

When you discover a feather, look beyond its intricate composition, feeling the message it bears. Does it show up at a time in your life when you are seeking answers to confusing or puzzling situations? The feather serves as a support system for you, indicating you are not alone in your quest.

Your Spirit guides and angels are right alongside of you each step of the way.

Guard the feather like a treasure. Put it on your altar, under your pillow, or carry it with you. Ask it to bring you the answer you are searching for. Trust it will connect you to your Spirit team, who will help solve your problem or provide you with the grounding you need to move forward.

The signs are readily available. When you slow your life down and enter a space of mindfulness, Divine communications are unmistakable. A bird song that catches your attention is calling to you. An unplanned event surfaces in your life, introducing your soul mate. The messages enter your energy field in a quiet fashion, calling you to notice them and interpret what they mean.

A shift in your consciousness initiates the process, harkening you to the mystical tokens. Remaining grounded and connected to Mother Earth, your awareness reaches a new level of perception. Performing service via prayer or meditation links you to Divine energy. These are important starting points to gain access to the symbols reaching out to you from beyond the veil.

Chills

Chills declare a Divine presence, affirming spiritual information from your helpers, guides, and angels. When chills appear in your energy field, they confirm what you believe to be true. An unambiguous feeling, chills infuse clarity into your awareness and faith.

Generated by energies other than your own physical thoughts, feelings and emotions, chills are a harbinger of Divine truth.

The chills began at age eight, when you began riding horses. A constant presence while interacting with us, your chills varied from experience to experience. While you had no conscious awareness of what they meant, you could feel their vibration moving up from the bottom of your spine to the top of your head.

As they reached your crown, the chills dissipated and vanished into thin air. Or so you thought. They were energetic signals, providing information about the Spirit realm, confirming the presence of your guides and angels as you navigated the formalities of the horse world.

Early riding school techniques were strict and rigorous. Hands and legs were required to be positioned in precise accordance with classical etiquette. There was no allowance for mistakes or misunderstandings. There was only one way to ride.

How carefully you were being watched! The chills were cold when you felt the restrictiveness around your body in relation to your horse. What mattered was the rigid structure which molded your body into a static form sitting on our backs.

The chills were warm and inviting when you groomed and stroked our faces. There were many horses at the school who felt this resonance with you. They responded sensitively, standing quietly, and inviting you into their energy fields.

You began to recognize the tingling feeling as a positive, affirmative connection to us.

Chills expanded the childlike wonder you felt in our presence. These were your indications of a deeper, subtler meaning around horses. Chills enabled an energetic connection beyond the physical plane, beckoning you to explore the Spirit realm. You felt the sonority between us.

Your journey with Spirit was unfolding.

The Hawk—a Messenger

There it was. An entire hawk carcass was laying in the grass on the hill outside the pasture gate. Magnificent, it was perfectly intact except its head was gone. Waiting to be discovered, you were astonished it hadn't been consumed by the local coyotes.

Why had it died next to our barn? Who had left it there to be discovered? Was it a deliberate action by another animal, waiting for you to find its carcass?

Replete with all its feathers, you carefully carried it into the house. A large hawk, its beauty was captivating. The shiny black and white feathers called you, asking for reverence and blessing.

The hawk symbolized an ingress to the Spirit world.

Its arrival was perfectly timed when you were just beginning to study the spiritual arts. Lodged in the old paradigms of the material world, your consciousness was unaware of the incipient portals which were opening for you. You were not yet attuned to the offerings from the Spirit realm.

Many years later you realized the hawk was a gift from Spirit. Its presence was there to support you on your path. Carrying messages of leadership, determination, clarity and protection, the hawk brought you animal medicine.

Spirit provided its own unique insight, sending the hawk as its messenger. When you understood the cosmic nature of Divine intelligence, you knew the hawk was unequivocal proof of Spirit's plan. A revelation, the entire encounter was Divinely timed. It was not some random accident which caused the hawk to perish next to our barn. The hawk's arrival was an ingenious spiritual maneuver.

To this day, you hold immense, heartfelt gratitude for the gift of the hawk.

Orbs: Monty's Spiritual Induction

The pose was ideal. My long, graceful neck wrapped around your body, a horse-human hug. The photo revealed our deep love and gratitude for one another. It was a perfect fit for the horse magazine article you were writing.

Since the picture was staged, I called in nature spirits to embellish the setting. We planned the time of day, guiding you telepathically to late afternoon. At dusk, the presence of orbs would appear in the camera lens.

A dozen orbs of different sizes showed up in the photo. Floating around the two of us, all of them were lustrous and shiny. The atmosphere was alive with their energy.

I was quite pleased with the outcome. Their dazzling light circled around us in the picture. But you were unhappy because it looked cloudy to you, believing your lens was dirty.

When you mentioned it to the editor, she said, "Look carefully at the picture. The spheres around you and Monty are not water spots on your camera lens. They are orbs."

You were astonished. When you consulted me, you learned orbs are allies from the Spirit realm, high vibrational emissaries who bring evidence of the unseen, an otherworld beyond the veil. Orbs manifest as round spheres of light, pearly and cloud-like forms. They appear translucent. In their vapor-like state, their shimmering, soft movement is undeniable, proving they are a tangible sign from Spirit.

Orbs contain volumes of Divine light. Floating effortlessly around the subject, they hover around the physical body waiting to deliver their message. Orbs have their own consciousness, choosing to manifest around individuals who are connected strongly to Source.

Orbs connect to the universal field of consciousness with invisible cords reaching deep into the atmosphere. While their messages are not written, their arrival highlights their notability. An orb's visitation signals a Divine blessing and protection.

Orbs affirm a metaphysical kinship.

Orbs may go unnoticed by the human eye. You must pay attention to their presence, or they will escape you. Their appearance is rare, but when it happens, there is no mistaking them.

Whether guardian angels hovering around you, or personal guides appearing in a bubble, orbs are mystical and magical occurrences. Orbs bring a message from another dimension.

Orbs appear when the sun is shining strongly in a natural setting. Like light rays, they materialize as reflective, transparent circles. Showing up around trees, water, or mountains, you may need to shield your eyes from their luminescence.

Orbs are visible at night when the stars are particularly bright. It is important to sense their energy in the sky. These orbs seem misty and can disappear quickly.

An encounter with an orb is an extraordinary experience, affirming how Spirit can touch your life in unimaginable ways.

Billy's Dreamtime Visit

You were troubled by the circumstances surrounding my death, believing we did not say goodbye. Witnessing my pain and struggle left you feeling helpless. With little notice or warning, my rapid demise and death were devastating.

Understanding your sorrow, I orchestrated a visit from the Spirit realm.

It was an auspicious night. You went to sleep, completely unaware of my plan. Our rendezvous took place on the astral, or dream, plane. I manifested in full physical form, my head as large as life. I appeared as vibrant as when I was alive.

When you felt my face next to yours, you woke up suddenly. Realizing I had been inches from you in the dream, you were hugely relieved. Your surprise turned into gratitude, knowing unequivocally I was there in nonphysical form.

My visitation proved with complete certainty to you I was complete. My countenance demonstrated the love I brought to you in dreamtime. When you woke up, you said, "Billy was here. He is OK. I am at peace, knowing he made a full transition to the Spirit world. He brought me a message to help me heal."

Dreamtime is a medium for Spirit-Spirit connection between the earthly and astral planes, affirming life beyond the physical world. This alternate reality unifies the physical and nonphysical realms. The dream state is an affirmation of life beyond death.

A dreamtime appearance is a spiritual confirmation.

Billy Gifts the Spiritual Cloak of Protection

As we prepare to leave our bodies, some of us convene with our angelic guides to manifest a gift for you. An energetic offering of great magnitude, we call this a spiritual cloak of protection. We place this absolute energy around your aura to help you perceive our presence, comforting you while you process your feelings of separation, sadness, and grief.

Millions of crystalline light shards are infused into the spiritual cloak of protection. While invisible to the naked eye, its radiance creates a vibration, like ripples of energy coursing through your body and field. Some of you may see the edges of an orb around you. When you feel tingles, it is we who are invoking the light-filled cloak.

Let the feeling envelop you in Divine love.

This cloak of protection is quite useful since you cannot see, feel, or touch our physical presence once we have crossed to the

Spirit realm. We hope you will learn to connect to our essence through journeying, energy transfers, visualization, prayer, meditation, or dream work, permitting the cloak to do its job.

Grieve not. Rest quietly inside the cloak, allowing it to assuage your heartache. If you concentrate properly, you can palpitate it, feeling it wrap soothing energy around you. Once you achieve self-actualization and the ability to tap into the Spirit realm, you will feel the cloak's power to generate an eternal connection between us.

Your personal cloak of protection is a powerful tool for alignment and change.

Monty's Precognitive Message

One day you asked me a direct question while we were riding. While you generated a thought, you spoke the words out loud. You said, "What will happen if you die before Romeo?" It caught me off guard because I didn't expect you to pick up on my ill health so soon.

It was a precognition, foreshadowing my death.

I responded immediately, saying, "Romeo will step up and become your partner." You wondered where the thought came from, but I sent it to you intentionally, timing it so you would understand my imminent crossing weeks prior to my physical demise.

A straightforward example of precognition, your thought manifested in the quantum before you uttered your words. An intuitive inkling, stirring our soul connection. A forewarning of impending events, precognition is a psychic phenomenon.

When you revisited the timing of my death, you understood you had an intuitive hit.

While you believed your question came out of nowhere, it landed in your conscious mind at the correct juncture. With the passage of time, you understood it was a warning sign. Your confusion was resolved once you saw the events unfold.

You and I were one soul when we were out riding together. Like other rides, you heard my words and knew unequivocally I was listening to yours. It was a two-way transmission.

When you get a premonition, your intuition is messaging you. Even if it doesn't make immediate sense to you, pay close attention. Trust Spirit to guide your feelings back to a place of safety until you can sort through the experience.

I know you were unprepared for my upcoming journey to the Spirit world; nonetheless it was already surfacing in your energy field. The thought emerged into your conscious mind, transferring to our communication. There it settled squarely in our conversation.

A psychic form of foreknowledge, precognition is a means to understand what may come, providing foresight into the future. Precognition is not necessarily a dire predicament. It can help you navigate uncertain information into a sensible plan of action, increasing your awareness to prepare for an unknown road ahead.

A tool for spiritual discernment, precognition is an important harbinger of change.

Monty Gifts the Aygu

After I died, I communicated the Aygu to you. This process was accomplished visually, where I showed the Aygu in the space behind your heart. It was a Divine activation, one which brought renewed peace to your grief.

The Equine Council created the Aygu for its use with horses. Our ancestors activated its presence, translating its messages through their stories and visitations. Many equine legends evolved from the Aygu's teachings. Equine strength and courage could be transmitted from horse to human via its power. Every type of human-animal spirit treasure is stored there.

A psychic space, the Aygu is an ancient mechanism through which horses and humans have communicated for millions of years.

Originating from the sacred star tetrahedron known as the Merkabah, the Aygu is an energetic entry point behind the physical heart. Like the Merkabah, it appears as a bright, semitransparent six-pointed star surrounded by a sphere. It can expand to fill your entire chest cavity with brilliant white light when activated.

A Divine creation, the Aygu contains memories from many lifetimes. It is an ongoing soul autobiography, a moment-to-moment account of your soul essence. The Aygu is filled entirely with high frequency love.

The Aygu connects your central nervous system and your endocrines to your thinking brain. It is so tiny even a microscope cannot detect it. Nourished by the love vibration, the Aygu's dynamism can be accessed by a thought or feeling. It is a magical sensation.

Then the Aygu's energy will fill your whole body with white light.

The Aygu's energy is activated from a place of pure quietude. Focusing your attention on it during a meditative state will magnetize its power, allowing the energy to flow directly into your aura. You will feel the Aygu expanding, opening our spirit-spirit connection. Like a still voice, you must be very quiet to hear it.

You will sense a soft movement in your chest, perhaps a tingling or a tickle. This is the awakening of the Aygu communication area. When your thoughts settle there, it's time to rest, and wait for a response. In complete silence, you will hear our voices talking to you. It's almost a whisper, but we will speak through this portal.

It is essential to keep the Aygu's portal active; leaving it dormant will promote a stale quality and it will become stuck. Emotions like grief, anger, frustration will linger in your heart center, making you vulnerable to disease and chronic conditions. Instead of holding on to heaviness in your heart space, you can redirect your feelings from grief to peace by kindling the Aygu's power.

Practice listening, and you will gain confidence about the Aygu's power. With persistence and patience, it will work for you.

A true dynamic force, the Aygu is an immortal energy, offering an unshakable connection between you and the Spirit world. With this knowledge, activate the Aygu at any time. Like a locket at the back of your heart, it is replete with Divine energy and love.

I taught you to feel my light in your Aygu's heart space, shifting it from sadness to joy. The images I sent you demonstrated how to replace the aching, grieving energy with the Aygu's light. The perceptible, almost touchable picture was tremendously reassuring.

Activating the Aygu in your heart space was an act of Divine grace. Its capability to expand and contract energy according to your thoughts, feelings, and emotions confers great power to you. It is the essence I grew.

A transference from the Divine to the physical plane, the Aygu's light can never be extinguished.

The Aygu

Romeo Calls in Wind Spirits

It was a gray, wintery day. The sun was hidden behind the clouds. The misty weather shrouded the neighboring mountains in fog. Even the crows and ravens were silent that morning while you cleaned the barn corrals.

In the hushed environment that day, you called up a simple prayer to heaven. "Spirit, please help me figure out the next step in my healing journey," you asked. A sense of peace was all around, with no noise or distraction to disturb your appeal.

In a split second, an intense wind tunnel rose from the ground. About 20 feet away, its swirling movement immediately caught your eye. A true force of nature, it behaved exactly like a mini tornado, storming furiously while kicking up dirt and rocks.

Immobilized, you watched as it whirled directly toward you. You wondered what would happen if it struck you. Would it knock you down or injure you in the process? You were frozen in awe.

Suddenly it made a sharp left turn, missing your body by a mere few inches.

A moment later, a second wind tornado emerged. As powerful as the first, it appeared for a reason. What was its significance? Was there a message for you? Its pattern was identical to the first, turning away from you seconds before it landed at your feet.

Now amazement set in as you hoped the two events were related.

When a third wind vortex spun toward you, the message became clear. The three were signals from the wind Spirits. Now it was time to interpret their appearances.

No doubt their trifold parade was correlated to your plea for help. They materialized immediately after your prayer. Their dancing energies were Divinely ordained.

A holy number, three was chosen intentionally to catch your attention.

A deep dive into the significance of the three wind tunnels revealed several messages. First, the number three was a sign of the holy trinity, supporting and guiding you. Second, the force behind the vortices substantiated the presence of the natural world. Their impetus got your immediate attention.

In a split second, Spirit showed up, shedding light on your query. The unconditional love and support you felt from your guides and angels was overwhelming. The three mini tornadoes which blasted toward and away from you were powerful signs from beyond the veil.

Wind power is a compelling manifestation of the Divine.

The Whoosh in the Wind: A Trail Riding Affirmation

Meandering along our favorite trail, the snow-capped mountains were particularly clear that autumn day. It was silent; only my hoofbeats made noise as we navigated around the trees and bushes near our barn.

Suddenly, out of nowhwere, you heard a distinct "whoosh" noise behind the nearby juniper trees. Stunned, you looked around for the source of the unusual noise. There was nobody there. You had a sense you were not alone, but a Spirit guide had joined our ride.

Indeed, you felt the presence of your Native American Chief, Mangos. While you did not hear his voice, you knew he gained your attention by the whoosh in the wind.

> *It was a moment of great clarity, a visitation without any deliberate action on your part.*

Wind is a powerful agent of Divine communication. When Spirit needs to get your attention quickly, wind spirits are summoned to deliver a message. Wind memos are short, swift and to the point.

A sudden burst of wind near or around you indicates a desire to speak with you. It may emit a sound, a crisp cracking noise from around a nearby tree or bush. Often these wind forms go unnoticed during weather changes or storms.

A wind tunnel is another active, energetic form. Delivering a specific message to you, it answers a plea or question you have put out to the universe. These tunnels look like mini tornadoes, swirling about rapidly while stirring up volumes of dust and debris from the ground.

Wind accompanied by a whooshing noise is a bigger delivery, indicating a direct visitation by one of your guides or angels. There is a clear ring to the rustling sound, especially when the environment is calm around you. When the whoosh arrives suddenly, it is a playful entry. While startling, it stops your day in an unmistakable way. Hearing this unusual noise emanating from a tree or bush means we are there, right by your side. The whoosh is a deliberate act of magic.

We have sent you wind tunnels and a whoosh to activate your sense of wind power. The tunnels occurred on a windless day in your corral, immediately after you raised your eyes to heaven and put up a plea for help. The whoosh surprised you one day while riding along the horse trail.

Paying attention to nature's movement gives many clues about Spirit's presence. Unexpected wind blasts and noise may be intentional actions to alert you to Spirit's presence. Shapeshifting itself into different vibrational frequencies, the wind shows itself in different ways.

A barometer, wind is an homage to the magnetic power of Source.

Part IV

Divine Truth

Chapter 11

Divine Truth

The quest for Divine truth is your birthright, a legacy you were born to explore. When you align with Source, its power is unequivocal. Divine truth is affirmative, proving without a doubt you are receiving spiritual intelligence. You recognize an unmistakable sensation in your body, affirming its presence. The energy of Divine truth is so strong nothing can rock its core.

Chills moving throughout your body validate Divine truth. Moving up and down your spine, they announce themselves with a cool, tingling feeling. Some rove about your legs, arms, and head. While they appear in an unannounced fashion, chills are the penultimate sign of Divine truth.

Opening an esoteric conversation with another person confirms a hallowed moment. An energetic shift in vibration in and around the physical body is evidence of Spirit's presence. The awe inspired by prayer, meditation and other forms of mindfulness will draw you closer to Divine energy, sanctioning the connection.

Through unmistakable messages, intentions and practices, Divine truths assemble in extraordinary ways. It does not matter how long you took to get where you are now, nor your chosen path. Your spiritual roots cannot be unearthed once you embody your soul journey.

Synchronicities unfold as if by magic. Like a pristine, clear quartz crystal growing from the Earth, all of life's goodliness and sacredness is contained in Divine truth. Your decision-making processes become easier than ever, drawing more light and love in your life. Taking on new clarity, circumstances are no longer random.

An overture of Divine truth, natural law ensues.

Identify and cherish your centering beliefs. Nourish them with all your being, trusting this knowingness supports you through life's challenges. By virtue of its unwavering power, Divine truth's rhythm coincides with your personal truth.

Finding your Divine truth is a monumental time in your life.

Your Divinity

Your Divinity is embedded in your soul. It is your complete connection to who you are in God's eyes, a sacred reflection. Nothing can take your sacred Divinity away from you, ever.

While your life path may lead you astray from the Spirit realm, you are never far from your Divinity. It goes where you go and does not need anything to activate its energy. It is ever-present and encompassing for your soul. You can return to Source at any time. Whether a life event brings you a new perspective, or you decide your current situation needs a makeover, it is never too late to recover your Divine essence. Source is a forgiving and non-judgmental essence, welcoming you into its embrace whenever you desire.

The portals to the Spirit realm are always open.

Your heart carries the core, impermanent Divinity you seek. This pure energy is sheltered in your soul even when external challenges seem to overcome your experience. We encourage you to enshrine your Divine self within your thoughts, feelings, and emotions, protecting it as if it were your child.

An endowment from Source, your Divinity is a precious and holy part of the absolute soul you are.

Your Divine Blueprint

Your soul has a predetermined roadmap, a Divine blueprint sanctified by universal law. Imprinted with its own distinctive acumen, your soul imports its Divine spark with it from lifetime to lifetime. An evolving process, the journey of your soul is ongoing, a primal blueprint.

Your soul carries your unique energetic signature. Before you incarnated into human form, your soul may have resided in the plant or mineral kingdom to prepare you for life as a human. As your Divine blueprint unfolded, you were birthed into different types of Spirits, learning important lessons along your path.

Each lifetime in which you reincarnate, you continue along your soul's timeline. No matter how many lifetimes you have spent in a human form, each one holds a new message for you. It is up to you whether you intuit your life purpose and fulfill its mission while you are in physical form.

Following your exclusive guidance will bring different challenges each time you incarnate. In some lifetimes, you will receive many blessings, in others, perhaps not. It is not a matter of how much abundance you have in your life; rather it depends on your relationship with the Divine and how you provide service to others.

As your guides, we can facilitate your blueprint organization. We support its unfolding, aiding where we are needed. This enables us to serve as your mentors, inspiring leadership decisions. We are your loyal servants in this capacity, encouraging your spiritual calling.

Chapter 12

The Soul

What Is Your Soul?

Your soul is an essential and indispensable part of your being. While you may believe your body is your wholeness, this is not the case. Your soul comprises more than ninety percent of who you are, thus making your physical self only a fraction of the consummate you.

It is said your soul can be present in seven bodies in the same lifetime. Your soul may be shared in multiple bodies. This piece of information makes life more exciting since you don't know if you are meeting up with other parts of you as you travel along life's timeline!

Your soul is a pure form of energy, continuing forth in a quantum state from lifetime to lifetime. Each time you reincarnate, you choose your parents, your life circumstances, and your soul path.

This is universal law.

Some of you understand these principles, applying them in your relationships and practices. Others continue in a more unconscious fashion, unaware of your soul's tremendous capacity for transcendence and peace when you sanction and bless your life's purpose. When you view your life from your soul's perspective, it opens many portals to the Spirit world.

The soul realm presents invitations to expand and transform your physical existence into an ethereal and impermanent version of reality.

The Light of the Soul

Windows to Your Soul

Like a mirror, your eyes emanate a reflection. They reveal the depth of your soul. Your soul's light contains a tremendous amount of information about its vibrancy, strength, and resilience. Like a looking glass, the light in your eyes reflect your soul's radiance and vitality.

Your soul's light can be quite bright, indicating a harmonious state of being. Dull or clouded light rays may reveal trauma, abuse, or sadness. Glistening or wavering light demonstrates a pause in your soul path.

The signs carried within are telltale.

We search your gaze for its messages. We observe how you carry yourself and whether you are a pure and genuine person. We can tell if you are in harmony with your soul, or not. This perceptiveness refines our mutual agreement, our contract.

Eager to greet you on a soul level, we await your response. We love to observe the wonderment and curiosity in your eyes. It is a desire to know and understand us on a deeper level. We are appreciative when you stroke our faces, watching how this relaxes our eyes.

We feel this vibration and we relay it back to you through our eyes. They will soften, filling with love, trust, and devotion. Then we will give our hearts to you, performing to the end of the Earth on your behalf.

Your eyes are the windows to your soul.

Soul Agreements

A soul contract is generated every time a horse and human enter into relationship. The union is blessed, bringing many conjoined experiences as the relationship evolves. Horse-human pairing is an integral part of a grand, quantum plan. Perfectly orchestrated, the match is Divinely ordained.

Each time we come into a new body, we offer our human an entirely new soul contract. If we choose to come back with you, the contract will have new and expanded lessons the two of us are learning together. We bring novel information along with us, helping you see things in a different light.

Soul contracts create new challenges and experiences.

It is an exciting prospect for us, especially when we choose to come back again with our human companions. A heartwarming emotion for both human and the horse.

Some of our contracts last a lifetime. This means we live out our lives with you until our physical bodies wear out. Other short lessons are absorbed and applied quickly. When the teachings involve deep and multilayered issues such as abandonment, fear, trust, or anger, these may take many lifetimes to assimilate.

We pass through and complete many phases together. Once our soul contract is complete, it is time for the horse or human to move on. This could mean a new partnership for one of us, or a choice to cross to the Spirit realm.

Soul agreements are an integral piece of our human-horse alliances. Replete with teachings, they have the potential to expand your understanding of why we come into your lives. Transcending the physical realm, your soul seeks its Divine blueprint. We guide the process, enveloping you into our soul collaboration.

Bear witness.

Death and the Soul Contract

The soul contract between human and horse cannot be altered. When the lessons are complete, you may shift the relationship by "selling" us to a new owner, making choices on our behalf which may or may not be beneficial for us. These decisions may or may not support our highest good.

Avoiding death and the ensuing pain it may cause to your loved ones is only a belief. Choices made using your free will might indeed recalibrate your life path. Yet, you enacted your destiny for birth and death prior to each incarnation.

You believe you can alter the timing of our death. Perhaps you mount a health intervention when we are critically ill, avoiding physical death. You suppose your decisions controlled the outcome.

You conclude you have control over death.

Your actions may save our life. The teachings are the important part. Maybe you changed our care, food, environment, or activity, enabling a better quality of life for us. Thus, this was part of the soul agreement between us.

In the case of illness, some decisions will guide you in a new direction. This can either improve or worsen our physical bodies, altering our destiny. Being aware of these choices is critical on the human side. It is ultimately our personal decision whether or not we will recover.

When physical death is not yet the intended outcome, the contract is not done. It may detour along the way, prolonging the human-horse kinship. Often the teachings are incomplete, leading the relationship further along its intended path.

While we do not enjoy needless suffering, we are not afraid to die. We understand what it means to live fully in the moment, facing death fearlessly. It is not a frightening process, but a natural progression in the limitless cycle of life.

From our perspective, death is not the end, but an opportunity to recreate a new body. Each lifetime we return with a new soul contract and purpose. Grasping the infinite nature of the universe, we embrace death as a welcome shift from one body to another.

We look forward to re-creating another body, often with our chosen soul mate. While we are in our transitional period in between lifetimes, we greet family and friends who have crossed before us. The period in between lifetimes is a spiritual reunion for us.

Since we can convene with those on the other side, we know who is waiting, welcoming us to the Spirit realm.

Impermanence

Your soul is impermanent, imperishable, and limitless. Its unique, invisible energy is transitory, finding a dwelling place in each body you incarnate. Your soul's intelligence is vast and omniscient, knowing no boundaries or limitations in its universal applications.

Your soul's immorality is central to your entire being. Its purity is untouchable, separate from the five sensory human body you inhabit. Nothing in the universe can damage or harm your soul. We understand this to be an immutable, natural, Divine law.

Your soul pilgrimage flourishes regardless of what takes place in your physical life.

After you leave your body, your soul remains intact until you select another physical incarnation. When you move from one physicality to another, it continues its journey.

While it may seem like a fleeting part of who you are, its boundless nature follows your Divine plan in a timeless continuum.

Regarding impermanence, you can learn a lot from us. We do not fear death, nor do we hold on to our physical bodies when they are finished serving us. We are eager to rejoin our loved ones in Spirit, carrying forth our mission with humanity.

A belief in the unseen power of the soul is critical.

The soul has a consciousness, and a desire to perpetuate its Divinity by remaining fully present in your energy field. Rather than remain in a vortex of grief and loss over your loved one's physical death, we encourage you to call upon the soul's ability to generate a vibrational exchange with us. Through psychic interactions with those who have crossed over, contact with the infinite soul is entirely reasonable and possible.

We understand physical death is not the end, nor does it indicate your relationships with your beloveds are finished.

Past Lives

Physical death is the end? We can assure you this is not the case. We reincarnate in any appearance, often returning to the physical plane as a recognizable figure. This is universal law.

We choose our birth, and we choose our death. We all have lived thousands of lifetimes, whether in a human, horse, or another form. While our bodies release their physical form when we die, our souls are eternal.

Because the soul is pure energy, its essence is recycled into the quantum field, returning in another form.

The belief you are a finite being dictates how you live your life, governing your personal freedoms, lifestyle choices and spiritual ascendance. You suppose you have ultimate control over your destiny.

To some degree, you do have control over how your life unfolds. You have the power of choice, which shapes your physical, emotional, mental, and spiritual health decisions. Healthy eating, positive thoughts, communicative relationships and connecting to Source are all tantamount to living the best life you can choose.

Each lifetime holds your karma. Your unfinished business prompts you to repeat your lessons until they have been accomplished. The residue from one lifetime must be resolved for you to reach another layer of transcendence. This is how past lives unfold, each banking on whether your karma from a previous incarnation is complete.

And so, your journey continues.

Authenticity

Your soul is the purest part of who you are in Spirit. No matter how you express yourself or live your life, your soul's infinite nature remains deeply connected to the Divine. Your soul has no hidden agendas, nor any self-judgments hindering its unfoldment.

Lifetime after lifetime, your soul is unblemished, embodying Divine light and love.

The path to authenticity is uncomplicated once you embrace your soul's innocence. Conscious of how your ego mind attempts to drive the decisions in your life, your self-perceptions shift. Vying for control, your ego may create stories and dramas to direct you away from your soul purpose but ultimately you will uncover your authentic self.

What are your self-sabotaging stories? Do you present as a truthful, honest human who acknowledges all sentient beings as equal co-creators of life on Earth? Have you discovered your true self as you are meant to be?

You are not always conscious of the untruths you tell yourself. You believe there are situations which merit your internal lies, leading to disparities in your relationships. These imbalances trigger negative programs, contributing to greater blockages in your life's energy.

Concede how and why you deceive yourself.

Honest self-assessment is an auspicious place to begin. Filter out the untruths, the false sense of reality you believe to be true. Then start approaching your life from a more genuine perspective. After this first step, reevaluate how you walk in the world, striding towards becoming a more authentic person. Drop the masks, honoring the self within who seeks liberation.

Moving from an unconscious to a conscious state of being once you achieve a state of honest self-assessment. New self-awareness enables you to expand your consciousness outside of your own energetic field. This new energy is invigorating, allowing you to interact with others in an entirely new fashion.

Then your authentic self will emerge.

Chapter 13

Healing

Abandonment

Every living creature on Earth understands the meaning of abandonment. The shock of being unexpectedly separated from one's pack, herd, or family may leave a deep imprint, creating distrust around life's uncertainties. As a result, prolonged trauma may ensue.

Abandonment may reach far beyond the physical into the emotional and mental realms. Starvation, isolation, and fear exacerbate any situation of loneliness and desertion. Whether horse or human, extreme forms of abandonment can even lead to death.

Like you, we carry the scars of abandonment. Consider us your ally; for many of us it is a familiar and recurrent theme in our lives, one we are willing to embrace on your behalf. We furnish the security of knowing you are never alone.

Together we heal from these experiences.

Surrender

Your human concept of surrender is one of defeat, relinquishing your power. It is interpreted as a failure, where you abdicate, forfeit, or give up something critical in your life. To you, surrender connotes capitulation to another person, event or circumstance.

In the equine realm, surrender means giving to the flow of life. It is not perceived as a loss. Rather, we define surrender as accepting life's challenges are an integral part of our soul path. It means allowing both pleasant and unpleasant experiences to unfurl in their natural order, accompanied by their teachings.

Surrender is easier than struggling to control situations we cannot manage. Going against the flow creates resistance and static, which makes life a struggle and blinds you to the joy all around you. Your problems are open doors for transformation, lifting you to a new level of awareness.

Release your expectations, clearing your resistance in energetically charged situations. When you disengage from anticipated outcomes, you permit life to unfold in its natural rhythm. We guarantee the ebb and flow of life will find its own pulse, pleasing you with its results.

Surrender is not acquiescence but allowance of all there is, the oneness of life.

Soul Healing

We understand the deep, unfathomable grief and despair you may feel when death occurs. The sense of personal loss can be completely devastating, leaving you feeling vulnerable and wounded. For some, death can leave you feeling unloved, betrayed, and lost.

Horse or human, we recognize these inner truths live within us. The grief state and its ensuing anger shed light on how they manifest in our lives, bringing them into our conscious awareness. If your soul woundings are buried in your unconscious, they can resurface when we die.

Death can stir up childhood issues such as abandonment, or lack of trust and protection.

We mirror these profound scars back to you, helping you acknowledge they exist. Nonetheless, grief may serve as a powerful healing tool. We call this soul healing.

The root cause of your grief stems from the absolute love you felt for another. This understanding will alleviate some of your inner suffering. Finding gratitude for the life you shared may also soothe your grief. Relying on others or us for unconditional love supports and comforts you.

Should you grieve for your equine partner, trust we will delegate another horse to step forth and continue with a new soul contract. We will not leave you in an unshielded or unprotected state; rather we will find a suitable replacement who will carry on our work with you.

Some of us have shared multiple lifetimes with you. You identify a complete familiarity about us; the reunion is unmistakable. Like an old friend, it is comfortable and easy to reacquaint.

Perhaps it is our legions of lifetime companionship with you which make it so much harder to say goodbye when we die. Your heartache is real, believing the end has arrived. Do not despair or cry for us because the ongoing soul connection remains intact, seeking healing from one lifetime to another.

We promise we will come back to you, lifetime after lifetime.

Heartbreak

From birth to death, life on Earth presents limitless opportunities to find meaning, love, and connection to your creator. This inner stamina is profoundly important. A belief in a benevolent higher power is crucial to your spiritual practice.

Your internal faith is called upon when an unexpected tragedy occurs in your life.

Your interconnectedness to one another builds strong communities, friendships, and companionships. Reliance on your human brother and sisterhoods helps carry you forth in hard times, fortifying your power as a human race. Your relationship with Source is the pillar of ultimate strength.

Suffering has its place in life's impermanence. Heartbreak offers an opportunity to examine the fragility of your human life, allowing gratitude and Divine support to lift your Spirit. Receptiveness to Divine guidance enables a return to wholeness. While the pain of heartbreak is inescapable in the human existence, the energy of love carries you forth into the infinite realm.

Out of your grief comes love, for had you not felt the intensity of your love, you would not have witnessed grief.

Chapter 14

Love

The Energy of Love

Love is the purest, most immaculate form of Divine energy. Sustaining all of Earth's creations, the love frequency reverberates at the core of the entire universe. More than any other vibration on the planet, love lifts your heart and Divine voice in resonance with heaven.

A musical matrix, love is the highest, most cohesive force in your existence.

Love's energy is a connector to the unseen realms, transcending time, and space. Key to your survival, love heals from the inside out while soothing your soul. Infinite in nature, love transfers powerlessness and vulnerability to strength and empowerment. When love adorns your relationships, it creates a magical perspective in your life.

Reinforcing the love vibration directs the unfolding of your life's passion.

Love is fundamental to your well-being, reaching deep into your energy field. It is a laudable and noteworthy goal for every human to discover love in his or her earthly relationships. Without love, the world would indeed be an empty, lifeless place to be.

With persistence and patience, love can override the deepest layers of suffering. Love can heal trauma, including physical, emotional, mental, and spiritual wounding. Once the pain is brought to the light, uncovered, and acknowledged, love is a curative force.

Love is the elixir for joy and the antidote to pain.

Living in the love vibration is a simple concept to understand, but it can be your most difficult challenge. Holding space for love means keeping your ego self in check as you relate to people and circumstances from your higher self, your soul. It means you surrender to your soul-self and move out of your own way for love to prevail.

An act of empowerment, evoking love's energy from your soul essence will benefit all of humanity and will come back to you repeatedly.

Your path is cleared. People and situations inspire and guide you toward the fulfillment of your potential and passion. In this state of being, you are heart-centered in thought, word, and deed. You project the high frequency of love and light, and it returns to you. This is the law of attraction.

You are in the flow of life. Your role shifts from reactor to responder. You are empowered.

When you can maintain a detached, neutral perspective, you can observe the drama others project onto you. Their stories do not belong to you. You emit love intentionally, sending light to those around you and for the benefit of the greater good.

Love will carry you through your darkest moments.

Putting love out vibrationally from your heart center is a conduit to the universal field. Life is the unfolding of a Divine plan, the evolving of Spirit within form. You are a co-creator, the architect of your soul journey.

The energy of love is indestructible. While feelings of unworthiness and brokenness stem from unfulfilled relationships, love remains the birthright of your soul. Sadness, grief, and heartbreak are often due to painful memories from the past. Like a hermetic seal, love is impenetrable and everlasting.

Living in the love vibration keeps us connected to the present moment, at one with ourselves and all there is.

Love versus Fear

While love is the highest energetic vibration, fear is the lowest. Fear springs from the unknown, an uncertainty of the future. Lack of trust, doubt, negativity, and anger can lead to a state of fear when you are stuck in an unstable or imbalanced relationship or situation.

Fear is often generated from a downward spiral of emotions as overwhelm sets in. When you feel you have little or no control over your problems, your fear seems insurmountable. Paralyzed, you may be unable to make a single move to change your circumstances.

Moving fear out and placing your trust into Spirit is a choice.

You are the captain of your ship. Guiding your thoughts, feelings, and emotions toward a higher power relieves the pressure you feel inside. Calming techniques such as meditation, prayer, breath work, yoga, chanting, and qigong calm your nervous system.

There you begin the process of surrendering to your fear, moving your awareness to a higher realm of consciousness. Yielding to your fear means identifying exactly what it looks like. Is the situation real, or illusionary? Is there a true crisis, or simply a foreboding sense of danger?

Using the power of "pause" provides a momentary break in the situation.

It takes courage to face your fear. Embracing it allows it to surface. Placing light directly on its cause encourages your fear to dissipate into the quantum field.

When you release anticipated outcomes, you allow life to unfold in its natural rhythm.

By releasing your fear to the unknown, you surrender to your circumstances. This acquiescence opens the doors for Spirit to do its work, importing signs and messages. Invoking faith in the Divine carries your energetic vibration into a space of acceptance, where all outcomes are possible.

Going into the void is a temporary solution and will be resolved as you follow the journey. In a space of nothingness, trauma has an opportunity to dissipate. You are protected in this silent, omnipresent force. It is a spiritual "container," where purity and Divine essence exist. At this moment you feel the power of infinite possibilities.

Fear cannot exist in the place of Divine, unconditional love.

Moving from a state of fear to trust can be challenging. An active practice, you are unwinding energetic patterns which hinder a spiritual life. You learn to harness the energetic power of your subconscious, changing your reality.

Consciously creating more love in your life lifts you to new heights, forming an unshakable bond with God.

Unconditional Love

The pinnacle of the love vibration, pure unconditional love is the very highest expression of the Divine. Holding its own unique frequency, unconditional love tones a more liberating and independent energy since it releases the love recipient of his or her responsibility to respond. Practicing this utmost form of the love vibration will assist you in freeing yourself from expectations or attachments.

Unconditional love does not anticipate narratives or outcomes; it is just a state of being in and of itself. Inseparable from your soul, it radiates from the heart. It is free from judgment and negativity. It is love without the emotional ties.

When you love without expecting an emotional return, your heart center expands, bringing in the same from others. It is a sheer joy to watch this unfold in your human world. We mirror this process back to you, encouraging you to imitate us. Unconditional love is a transformative power.

If unconditional love were to be withdrawn, the entire universe would immediately collapse in an instant.

Unconditional love is an integral part of your collective human experience due to its expansive and pervasive nature. Others around you receive and assimilate the vibrations you are emitting, responding accordingly. They will become happier and more peaceful around you.

Unconditional love liberates you from the ego's influence, conveying unlimited freedom. Treating others with the love of non-judgment, compassion, forgiveness, and understanding releases your soul, connecting you to the universal field where love prevails. An integral part of your human consciousness, its Divine truth sustains the entire universe in all spheres of life.

Unconditional love is the very energy behind all creation.

Chapter 15

Empowerment

The Magic of Manifesting

The genesis of manifestation is intention, a feeling so strong you can visualize exactly what you wish. Manifestation means you can effectuate the outcome by using specific techniques to bring your conscious dreams into actualization. Manifestation is the embodiment of your deepest wishes, bringing what you desire into your physical reality.

> *Manifestation is a co-creative force, merging your personal vibrational signature with universal energy.*

Carrying a pulsating charge, your conscious thoughts are entangled in the collective consciousness. Whether positive or negative, they do not operate in a vacuum. An evolving energy, your soul works directly with Source to attract what you want.

The first principle of manifesting is to practice positive thinking in every facet of your life. Allow unpleasant thoughts to drift in, then shift them towards your highest good. Utilize the unpleasant experience as a lesson, taking what you need from it. Injecting a sense of humor to diffuse the negative spin into a brighter, more colorful vibration.

Second, set your intentions in the most realistic and constructive manner. Maintaining a lighthearted attitude will remove the pressure, ensuring a better energetic flow. If there is any doubt in this space, it won't work. Remove the doubt by grounding it to the center of the Earth via a grounding cord or simply asking your guides to expel it from your energy field.

Third, visualize the goal you have in mind. Express it with strong, clear words and pictures. Believe it with your heart and soul, activating it as if it has already occurred. You feel the "energetic click," as the vibration grabs hold. Chills appear when your goal has been implanted securely in your energy field.

Fourth, call upon your personal guides for help. Tell them what your goals and inspirations represent. You do not need to do this alone. Even if you do not know who your guides are, trust they will show up and help you when you ask.

You are manifesting the events in your life whether you are aware or not. Your thoughts are constantly running through your mind, directing energy in and out of your field. So even if you are not "thinking" about how you operate in each moment, your subconscious programs affect your life's events.

Your intentions spring to life when your energy is commingled with The Divine.

True Power

True power originates from within your soul. Nonphysical in nature, it has great potential to influence your conscious thinking and your free will. True power is magnetic, calling you to investigate its life-changing qualities. Ultimately, embracing your soul's inner strength will facilitate your transcendence to the Spirit realm.

True power has nothing to do with the money or possessions you accumulate, the level of success measured by your societies, or whether you influence others in your life.

True power should not be used in a negative fashion, abused, or wasted. Misuse of power for personal gain will block your path, shutting down your access to the Spirit realm and damaging your relationships. Acknowledging your inner resources will reinforce your connection to Source.

This allegiance to your core beliefs allows your purpose to unfold, bringing the faith and devotion necessary to remain in complete calibration with your power. You recognize nothing can prevent you from fulfilling your destiny. When you discover your purpose in this lifetime, you will find a peace unlike any other.

True power means you align yourself with the all-knowing, Divine matrix of creation.

Grounding

Grounding is a tool to refresh and reset energy. It accesses the Earth's deepest core where the magnetic power of Source is stored. Grounding links your vital force with earth energy, releasing pessimistic thoughts, feelings and emotions.

Horses create four grounding cords that extend from the bottom of our hooves into the center of the Earth. We invite this energy to ascend through our legs, into our midsections and out the top of our heads. From there we draw down cosmic energy from the galaxies and stars into our field, blending the two spiritual powers.

Grounding reinforces our internal resources.

You can employ these same methods with your bodies. It is identical except for the difference in body shapes. Using your foot and crown chakras as receptors, just ask your personal earth and cosmic energies to flow through you. Merging them along your spinal chakras, you are calling earth energy into your field. Like a click, this feels solid and strong.

Grounding is an easy procedure, one which cleans out your energy field. Nourishing your aura, it clears stagnant energy and recycles it back into the Earth's center. Grounding is a powerful tool for releasing anything that does not serve your highest good, such as toxic thoughts, behavior, and actions.

We can pass our grounding energy to you whether you are on our back or not. Receiving its power through these channels enables us to relay energy through our bodies to yours, and let it go. Simply being in our presence will have the same effect.

Because grounding is a soothing and quieting feeling, it is desirable to practice this skill frequently.

Forgiveness

Your human thoughts and words have the capacity to deliver hurtful messages. The brunt of your frustration and anger has been directed at others. Your antagonistic, resentful feelings may endure beyond their initial impactful events, creating lasting trauma for some of you.

The enmity in your human projections reflects unresolved inner conflicts within your soul. You feel sad, confused or betrayed when someone you love and trust treats you in an unjust or wrathful manner. Taking it personally, you react in kind, sending the same unloving messages back. Focusing on the negative, toxic energy builds, creating an unforgiving blockage in your relationship.

These long-term grudges create a spiral effect, where you interpret new experiences in a negative light. Assuming you are the victim, you assimilate the pain and suffering from past emotional unraveling. You forget your ability to stay present and connected to life's positive flows.

Rather than allowing the pain to remain inside, great healing can occur. Releasing your suffering, your soul is liberated. Finding equanimity, choose to put your traumas into perspective. Finding forgiveness in your heart is the practice we recommend.

Finding compassion and understanding for a situation or individual who has hurt you benefits your soul.

Forgiveness can be a formidable task, especially if the person who has hurt you doesn't admit their misstep. For some of you, this may be challenging. We encourage you to take a higher road toward a peaceful solution.

Start with empathy. Invite compassion and wisdom for another's mistake. In this process, you may uncover a middle ground where both parties regret their words and actions, resulting in reconciliation. You feel and understand the pain of another to heal and bring them back to their true selves.

Empathy helps you have a clearer vision of what you want to achieve, which is a more loving and easier relationship.

You can ask for forgiveness on the soul level when communication breaks down. Tell the other party you are very sorry and regret your words or actions. This will be received, even if it does not land in the physical plane.

A personal tool for peace and harmony, forgiveness calls your power back to you. Grounding and centering yourself in the space of forgiveness are the essences your soul desires. A return to wholeness, you realign your principles with Divine truth.

Holding the loving light for others, forgiveness begets compassion, empathy, and respect.

Gratitude

Gratitude magnifies your soul consciousness, drawing you close to your life blessings. It reminds you to acknowledge the Divine in the mundane. Surrounded by universal energy, gratitude accesses the quantum force field, tapping into its creative power.

The universe loves gratitude.

Gratitude begins on the soul level, an appreciation for the goodness within and around you. By focusing on the positive blessings all around you, you raise your vibration to one of joy and balance. Like other practices that cultivate your Divine consciousness, gratitude embellishes your personal signature, enabling you to make sweeping changes in your life.

Gratitude holds a highly vibrational frequency. It brings a tremendous amount of light into your field. The more you practice gratitude, the higher level of happiness can be achieved. A harmonic, peaceful state of being, gratitude strengthens your positive emotions.

Having a hearty dose of gratitude in your heart enables you to face hardships with a different perspective. Rather than feeling victimized, you can overturn difficult situations. When you activate the power of choice, your decisions will target your desires.

Gratitude filters out toxic energy.

A non-dual essence, gratitude benefits the greater good. Whether this is a thought, action, good deed or prayer, energy is directed toward universal healing. Your contribution is paid forward to others in need of Divine grace, emitting a loving vibration the cosmos will receive.

Carve out the time to infuse gratitude into your daily practices. Using prayer, meditation, or mindfulness tools, pause and reflect on the goodness in your life. Whether your gratitude springs from your own healing path, or honoring others who have helped you along the way, it need not matter. Give thanks for all your blessings, feeling your soul respond with a feeling of fullness and joy.

Practicing gratitude brings light into your life, generating greater spiritual resilience.

Reverence

When you embrace the magnitude of Divine power, a sense of reverence unfolds. The matrix of creation is at play, affirming the interconnectedness of all beings. Surrounded by a feeling of wonder, you recognize how reverence stirs in your soul.

The universe has its own innate, holographic intelligence. Operating beyond the human measurements of time and space, its rhythm operates on a quantum level, connecting each soul into its field. Whatever vessel you inhabit, accessing this universal energy is your Divine birthright.

In a reverent moment, you acknowledge the universe's multidimensional nature, where no single creature stands alone.

This vast pool of cosmic information is ever-present in your cellular matrix, flowing through your body. Available in waking and dream states, its network is infinite. Its Divine qualities grant permission to tap into its power, transforming energy from one state to another in your personal energy field.

Resting in this reverent state, you perceive your world through a different lens. Unlike the religious texts, reverence does not mean fearing your creator. Nor asking for favors from deities, saints or angels. Spiritual reverence means complete and unconditional respect for the glorious, multifaceted quantum reality that grants your life.

Practicing deep, unconditional love and respect for all living beings defines reverence. A symbiotic relationship with each breathing being in the universe and the Earth herself holds you in a reverent state. This is the quality of a high vibrational relationship with God.

Reverence bathes you in Divine light, expanding life's ultimate sacredness with all the beauty it holds.

Faith

Your personal spiritual journey starts with a foundational faith in the Divine. This conviction indicates complete trust and confidence in Spirit's ability to organize and govern the universe. All your thoughts, emotions and actions are guided in relation to God.

Coupled with an active service to others, the pervasive, ubiquitous power of Source permeates all of creation, providing a constant flow of information and support. Your belief in Spirit must be unwavering and nonnegotiable. Whether religious in nature or not, faith operates in the universal field to bring all souls together for the betterment of humanity.

At its deepest level, faith is rooted in the knowledge that everything happens for a reason. It assumes good will prevail over evil, even when life brings you hardships or challenges. Faith extends beyond hope, relying on your human-Spirit connection.

Faith sustains and supports you.

Belief opens channels to receive information when you are facing difficult times. Turning your worries over to your Creator unblocks your answers, illuminating what you need to know. Believing everything will resolve positively is helpful, even when you lose hope.

A profound, faithful practice works on the cellular level, coursing through your endocrines, nervous system, and organs.

Developing a faith-based practice has many benefits. Using your mind to generate energy, you create a state of positive thinking. This expands your faith into a state of wholeness with all of creation, bringing more abundance in your soul.

Bringing strength to your physical and emotional bodies, faith is critical for a complete spiritual existence.

Faith

Chapter 16

Energy

Vibration

All living beings are pure energy, each with their unique, vibrational signature. Starting at the subatomic level in the body, your thoughts, feelings, and emotions create a symbiotic relationship with your cells that determines your physical health. At this energetic level, cultivating positive energetic patterns is not only essential to good health; it is key to creating the most spiritually attuned frequencies.

Known as the aura, your vibrations flow in and out of your bodies at different frequencies, pulsating with your own energetic output. Connecting to Source, vibration is eternal. Thus, yours cannot be destroyed, so it is important to keep it functioning at its highest potential. Hence the term, "like attracts like." Your vibration will attract more of the same, whether positive or negative.

Your personal frequency is unique. It is not separate from another's, but engaged with the infinite, timeless Divine matrix. What you do not only affects you, but all others.

Vibration establishes your reality, affecting every aspect of your life. It enables a state of resonance, or harmony with your soul and the Divine.

Universal Energy

Your soul's journey belongs to you. Nourishing your soul is part of the healing process you pursue. Nesting into its own unique place in the universe, your soul seeks wholeness.

Universal Energy

Championed by your intuition and free will, you choose to engage in the magic of the Spirit world. An infinite reality, you align yourself with its magnetic power. The grand design unfolds, bearing information about your role in the whole of creation.

Transformation takes place in the realm of universal energy.

Horses perceive the universe as an eternal dimension outside the confines of time and space. A unified field of consciousness, vibration and frequency enables energetic coherence among all living beings. In this holographic domain, there is no division among you. Your collective soul essence flourishes in a timeless amphitheater.

This is the quantum reality.

In the quantum field, your personal energetic signature works in tandem with the Divine plan. All vibrations seek resonance and organization. Your body, mind and soul are inextricably entwined into the infinite matrix of energetic coherence, a Divine natural law which governs all creation.

Your individual reality is circumscribed by the frequencies you emit. Nurturing your connection to all other souls and your creator, you are part of the oneness. This universal Source energy is the wellspring of your core spiritual essence.

From the primordial level of human existence to your soul's everlasting continuum, we recognize everything is energy.

Entanglement

In the quantum field, how you think and behave affects every other soul in the entire universe. On this level, there is no vibrational division among you. There is no duality energetically because all vibrations are commingled in one impermanent, universal field of consciousness.

Also known as the oversoul, this cosmic vibrational force is unencumbered by time and space. It is a matter of Divine law, functioning outside the confines of your physical reality.

Horses thrive in the quantum realm. We intuit Earth's electromagnetic fields, feeling weather and atmospheric shifts. We are cognizant of the changes in your collective human experience long before they manifest in your reality.

These pulsations show up as vibrational inputs in our energy fields, allowing us to decipher valuable energetic information. Our ability to interpret and pass along these signals is one of the most important concepts in the equine world. The earthly vibrations we recognize may bring warning signs to you.

Whether the Earth's messages manifest as hurricanes, droughts, earthquakes, or global pollution and warming, they are increasing in nature. It is something we are trying to teach you as we work with you on the earth plane. This knowingness helps us prepare for your wars, your economic upheavals, and your destructive weather patterns caused by human waste and pollution.

On both the micro and macro levels, pay attention to the frequencies within your energy field and the emissions they put out. Starting with your thoughts and actions, ensure they are of right intention. Then release the pure ones into the quantum field.

Knowing all of this will help you align your personal energetic frequencies with Gaia. She will feel your intentions of "do no harm," honoring your part to keep your individual vibrations in synch with the universe and all other beings. In this mode of entanglement, you will access all the metaphysical and sacred information available to you.

Entanglement enables you to embody a fully spiritual existence, one in resonance with Spirit.

Intention

Intention begins with an unconscious impulse. Unaware of what is ruminating in your subtle energy field, it desires to surface. By the time you have a conscious thought, your mind has created a motive to act. Conscious reasoning creates energy, and energy follows thought.

A framework for intention, your mental and emotional attitudes impel your energy.

Since intention turns into action, it is critical to direct your thoughts, feelings, and emotions toward the most creative, productive outcomes. With unambiguous energy, direct your intentional impulses toward exactly what you desire. Do not allow any unwanted beliefs or sentiments to permeate your objective.

In this manner, you will be able to form a clear channel for your intentions to manifest. Whether it involves your relationships, your career, or your service to the Spirit realm, keep your focus unhindered and pure. This is the means to making energetic desire work in your favor.

Be mindful. Energy cannot be destroyed. Once your mindset is projected into the quantum field, you will attract more of the same vibration, whether positive or negative. Honor and guard your energetic intentions, cherishing their value as if they were your best friends.

Intention is your vibrational output. It directs the outcomes that follow your thoughts, feelings and emotions. Setting clear and awe-inspiring intentions is indispensable for your physical, mental, spiritual, and emotional health. Pure intention is one of the highest energetic states you can achieve.

Embrace the energy of intention's power with your whole being.

Chapter 17

Transcendence

Portals to the Spirit Realm

The portals to the Spirit world are always open. You are welcome to enter through these doors and discover your guides, angels, nature spirits, helpers along with all the signs and signals you desire to build a connection to the Divine. Source energy can be ignited when you put your attention on it.

It is never too late to accept Spirit's invitation to you.

Many of you go through an actual initiation. You are invited via your guides to join in complete silence where pure Spirit resides. This serenity brings oneness in mind, body, and soul. Horses know intuitively how to do this because we are in constant connection, reach and understanding of how to go within and find our answers within our innermost souls.

To access this realm, ask. When you begin seeking answers to the infinite source of consciousness and the all-knowing Divine energy, your energy field expands. Guidance will touch your soul.

Be open to this invitation. We have much to offer you as your companions, friends, and spiritual teachers. We willingly lead you to a blissful and quiet realm of spiritual ascension. Summon us to join your journey.

Navigate the Spirit realm with us. Pure energy resides in the merger of mind, body, and soul. Accessing profound stillness and calm transports you to a different reality, one where the line between you and "other" ceases to exist. You are in the quantum field of unified consciousness.

Equanimity

In a state of equanimity, all illusions of separateness and isolation fall away. Placing your complete trust in God, you experience a greater order to the universe. Releasing all attachments to your physical world enables you to sense the Spirit realm around and within you.

You may feel alone when solely convening with Source, but you are not. Surrounded by your Spirit team, a sense of protection unfolds. Reaching a state of non-reactiveness, you access an equanimous zone with an open and receptive mind. Your disturbing thoughts, feelings are grounded out of your aura, exchanging them for calming and neutral ones.

The sphere of equanimity quiets the anxious, future oriented mind. It permits you to detach from a chaotic and unstable world. Where there is suffering, you also find blessing. Where there is trauma, you also find healing.

Equanimity is the middle ground amidst the universal, energetic polarity, helping to heal the separateness in your human reality.

When you live your life in a neutral way, judgments of self and others fall away. Without criticism, you become a more temperate person, allowing your being to unfold. Less reactive and more responsive to life's ups and downs, personal power resides in an equanimous state of being.

Your human mind is a very busy one, creating perpetual drama and stories. Equanimity holds you accountable for your beliefs and actions while pursuing your meaningful passions. It is a state of being whole with yourself, no matter what life circumstances you are facing.

The quantum field is accessible in a state of equanimity, illuminating your Spirit path.

Silence

All beings have a great capacity to communicate in silence. While your spoken words carry enormous influence within your human communication, the silence between them reveals more power than the words themselves. An energetic pause, silence provides the means to communicate telepathically.

Silence reaches deep into the soul, accessing the quantum field in an informational exchange.

You frequently relay mixed messages. Speaking in a double tongue, your messages are veiled. You anticipate direct communications might appear hurtful or harsh, saying one thing while meaning another. Instead of delivering your words in a gentle and clear fashion, your conversations emerge in a convoluted way.

Silence manifests in the form of your thoughts, your emotions, or feelings. It's in our breath, our eyes, and our body language. It is an invisible communication between two beings, crossing the energetic lines.

Horses communicate nonverbally with energy. Clairaudience is one of our primary means of sending and receiving messages. We feel the vibrations emanating from our field and can project them toward one another.

Imagine using a thought to make your point. It is the power of your thoughts and emotions we perceive. When you are excited, we can sense this without words. Whether you are happy or sad, we react in kind.

Silence acknowledges deep emotions and feelings without a verbal exchange. Working in silence forges a symbiotic relationship, a give and take between us. Silence operates without words, thoughts, or emotions.

Silence expresses the soul.

Heightened Awareness

The universe provides messages and meanings for your life. Sharpening your five senses of sight, smell, sound, taste and touch, your perceptions shift to the subtle energies that surround you. By observing the natural world, you raise your awareness of the Spirit realm.

Heightened awareness expands your energy field. A wake-up call, it taps into the invisible, subtle way of understanding who you are. Dropping the illusion of your ego self, your consciousness shifts to a higher perspective. In this zone, you are connecting to the ethereal energies all around you.

Your individual thoughts, feelings and actions are pooled into the all-encompassing Source arena, joining all of us together in a non-dual universe.

Heightened awareness has its own navigation system based on connecting to the quantum field. You enter the field of universal consciousness, where every thought, action, feeling, emotion is connected. Here all souls are connected in the oversoul, where there is no division.

Accessing the quantum through heightened awareness connects you to the Divine.

To activate this state, note the signs and sounds from the sun, wind, clouds, water, trees, animals, insects, and any other member of the Earth's vast communities. You are tapping into the unseen mysteries of how the field operates. These signs are present every waking and sleeping moment of your life on Earth.

A state outside conscious thoughts and actions, heightened awareness does not operate from your physical senses. When you access universal energy, life's synchronicities unfold, affirming nothing is coincidental, or random. Threads emerge, creating a magical tapestry. Sensing the invisible energy around you will thrill and amaze you. Your observations now bring new clarity, bearing unmistakable clues of synchronicity and meaning.

Spirit has been by your side all along.

Tranquility

Tranquility brings a state of complete surrender and peace. Corollary to stillness, tranquility produces an air-like sensation, almost as if your physical body has melted into the atmosphere. Receptive to the signs outside your five senses, your soul is in complete alignment with the Spirit realm.

You achieve a state of unity with the Divine.

Your thoughts, emotions and feelings are quieted, almost to a complete standstill. Setting healthy boundaries to protect and cherish this sacred arena keeps you centered. Using breath, gentle movement, and grounding, you reset your vibrations to match the earth frequencies.

A state of tranquility revitalizes your energy.

Discovering a tranquil state is not difficult to accomplish. Imitate us, watching how we give off big release breaths to help us slow down physically. Then our vibrations recalibrate. Tranquility is our preferred means of restoration since it is our nature to seek body, mind, and spiritual attunement.

We encourage you to develop this practice. Finding a centering breath to begin, follow your breath until you feel a sense of serenity in your body. Continue until your thoughts slow down, and your focus can remain on your breath. Do this for 10–15 breaths, calming and resetting your nervous system.

Tranquility can bring peace and harmony into your life. It will restore your sense of balance and connection to the quantum field. In this dimension, you will understand the infinite nature of your soul, discovering a glimpse of eternity.

Non-Duality

The concept of non-duality is one of our favorites. We are spiritually qualified to bring you the information, helping you shift your perception from a place of separateness to one of unity. This may be difficult to understand without resorting to your scientific theories about quantum mechanics, so we use energetic language to explain our interpretation of non-duality.

According to Divine plan, everything in the universe starts with energy. Energy is always moving, seeking resonance, alignment, and ultimate coherence. On a soul level, your individual energetic blueprint is inextricably linked to the cosmic oversoul, the universal consciousness.

Each of you has a unique connection to this quantum matrix, bringing your body-mind-soul self into accordance with all others. Every one of Earth's creations also resides there, enabling you to reach deep into their soul essence when you wish to align with them. This means there is no separateness on the energetic level, making the web of interdependence and connection reach cosmic proportions.

Eternally linked to the Spirit realm, non-duality is the process of becoming connected and whole.

There is truly no separation or dual consciousness. We project our thought frequencies into the quantum, landing in a giant pool of consciousness. The vibrations can be felt. Telepathically received, our feelings and emotions become vibrational outputs. This energetic connection goes beyond time and space.

The phrase, "be careful what you wish for," is a truism for humankind.

We live in non-dual reality. We do not understand your separate, binary world. We watch how you alienate your fellow humans through your anger, and your judgment of how others live their lives.

Your harsh destructive actions like war and murder leave us wondering how you have survived as a species.

Your journey to wholeness begins on the inside. As sparks of the Divine, we carry its light within. Seeking unity, we wish to repair the broken or imbalanced parts of our soul. Unity is a spiritual birthright, achieved by living in the love frequency.

There is no separation ... we are all sparks of the living God. What affects one, affects us all. Wholeness, on the other hand, means being complete as an individual, and in harmony and balance on all levels of being—body, mind, and Spirit.

To be whole means to gather up and heal our fragmented pieces—the parts of ourselves which are disconnected from Spirit.

Your Spirit Team

Your Spirit team is comprised of many guides, nature spirits, ancestors, and angels. They rotate in and out of your life, some providing consistent advice and others appearing less frequently depending on specific circumstances. Some stay with you for your entire lifetime; others are temporary guides who show up and help you resolve a problem.

You can reach out to your Spirit team at any moment you desire. They are only a thought away.

You have a Master Guide, sometimes called a Healing Master. Your Healing Master has many duties, including ensuring all your spiritual inquiries are directed to the appropriate advisor.

It is likely your Healing Master has been with you many lifetimes, supporting your soul's evolvement.

Other important titles in your Spirit team include joy guides, Spirit doctors, and philosophers. These tertiary guides are incredibly helpful in daily activities, including decision making. Sometimes one of us in Spirit serves as your guide, making our presence known in dreams, visualizations, and meditations.

Angels are in a completely different category than your personal guides. While we know each one of you has at least one Guardian Angel who walks by your side every moment of your life, the Archangels who serve mankind on both an individual and collective level are available in a moment's notice to help you in any given situation. Angels like to be called, so ask them for help when you need their support.

Your physical homes and surroundings house nature Spirits who reside in the mountains, water, trees, ground and even the rock formations. The gnomes and fairies listen and respond to any query you have. It is always wise to consult them before you begin a home improvement project, such as landscaping your property or chopping down a tree.

They are sensitive to their environment and prefer to be alerted to any impending change to their homes.

Horse energy serves as a bridge between the human and Spirit realm. We are ambassadors, backing your Spirit team to function effectively. We embody strength and power, so we carry this energetic resonance for you when you desire to reach your team members.

Call upon our medicine to activate your light codes, bringing clarity to all your Spirit team relationships.

Angelic Guidance

Angels are a source of Divine presence. Made of pure energy, they are the closest form of Divine essence we acknowledge. They vibrate at a high rate, allowing them to travel quickly when they are needed.

You are always surrounded by the presence of angels, both your personal ones as well as the ascended masters known as the Archangels. They are available to help you with a thought, feeling or action. They will never abandon you, even if you have abandoned them. Their love is always forgiving, allowing you the trials and errors of human life.

The high frequency light that angels emit draws you into their energy fields. Resonating a feeling of pure love, they may announce their arrival with chills, a breeze, or a flash of light. Their presence will envelop you, shifting your emotions into a celestial sphere of hope, love, and healing.

It is important to establish angelic assistance by invoking their energy. They desire to hear your appeals, asking for their help in any situation. They will respond to you in a way you will understand.

As light bearers, horses are supremely connected to our angels, nature spirits, and elementals. We feel their keen guidance in our lives. While we do not pray or ask for assistance in the same way you do, we understand that our helpers are available to us.

Angelic love reaches all of us on Earth.

Freedom

Illuminating the Divine spark within your soul is an auspicious juncture in your life, leading you to a life of spiritual freedom. Reaching this goal may take multiple lifetimes to achieve. With guidance from your team of guides, angels, nature spirits and ancestors, your momentum builds each lifetime. Using the power of intention, your awareness will automatically heighten as you take steps toward achieving a newfound sense of freedom.

Noting this is a process, the layers of transformation will come at their own pace, showing up in your life when you are ready. Nothing is coincidental; every alteration in your vibration is met with a synchronous response from the Universe. Once you have cohered to a direct and unequivocal practice of Divine connection, the gateposts and signs are unambiguous.

Clearing old problems makes room for others to surface. Rest assured you are not backpedaling. While invisible, your soul continues to ascend according to your Divine blueprint. You feel your spiritual growth as you notice more equanimous reactions to issues that previously upset you, developing a heightened awareness around your life in a new way.

Your soul seeks the freedom that circumscribes your physical existence since the beginning of time.

You become conscious of the changes that transpire in your personal "freedom" space. The shifts will bring both excitement and uncertainty. Be confident your feelings are normal; it is part of the human way to feel the push/pull of your existence.

The sum of all the changes will produce a new sense of awe and glory, indicating your role in a greater universal holism. While you are one individual, your work on the soul level is collective. Together you will make a difference in the greater good as you develop the skill set to integrate your personal essence into the Divine oversoul.

Balance and harmony flow naturally in the realm called spiritual freedom.

Part V

The Triune Concludes

The Golden Hue of Pure Consciousness

Light bearers are those who pursue a Spirit path, believing in the power of Divine love and light to help heal the Earth and its inhabitants. They devote their life to service, upholding the Divine spark in their thoughts, feelings and actions. Their path is mindful, quietly encouraging all to discover the magic and wonder of the Spirit realm. All sentient beings can find this calling in their quest for enlightenment.

The application of light work can be seen in a visualization. Known as The Golden Hue, shards of light are organized into a breathing, living organism. Like beautiful rays of sunshine, its brilliance radiates from the inside out, inviting those who bear witness to it to feel its warmth and comfort.

There are no limitations, boundaries, or constraints in the field of pure consciousness. Within this infinite realm of the soul, all healing is possible. The physical coalesces with the nonphysical. A supreme blend of your wholeness, you expand beyond your body to access information from all space and time, without the parameters of the physical reality.

The Golden Hue stores your soul's imprint and coding since the beginning of time.

The Golden Hue appears when you enter a place of silence, purity, and deep spiritual connection. Activated when you are in our presence, it creates a state of stillness between horse and human. Our energy fields become one, encircling us in its orb, unified in a non-dual energy.

The Golden Hue is a mystical force. Its crystalline light is a sign of transcendence, representing your deep commitment to the Spirit path. Through reverence, gratitude, and faith you manifest this iridescent light, embodying its Divine intention.

With transcendence as your goal, The Golden Hue creates a state of heightened awareness and understanding that brings you ultimate peace.

The Caduceus of Love

A compelling symbol of love, the caduceus can be conceived between any two beings on Earth. Like the serpents and staff logo, the caduceus generates an upwards and downwards flow, intertwining and merging our heart chakras. Once our heart chakras are blended, the caduceus energy reaches up to the heavenly realm where Divine light is omnipresent.

Your third eye or brow chakra can generate the image of a caduceus. It embeds in and around your heart space until the end of your soul contract with one another. While the caduceus figure is palpable, its energy is ethereal, making it a powerful love activator.

Unlike any other figure of love, the caduceus is supreme in nature.

The caduceus power can be destabilized. Since it is connected to your heart chakra, sad or depressed feelings may sever it from Divine energy. Disengaged, the caduceus malfunctions, blocking light from your heart space.

When your heart chakra is closed, you cannot access inner compassion, nor perform your work on Earth. You cannot feel your own emotions or even begin to find any loving memories because of your grief. The joining of the caduceus serpents is blocked, and your heart is shut down.

You cannot momentarily find or share Divine love, nor feel light from Source. Your ability to modulate or perpetuate the light you carry within is temporarily closed. This is why it is so important to understand the grieving process, so you can return to a space of love.

Due to the soul's impermanence, our place in your heart transcends time and space. Via the caduceus symbol, its light can grow dimensionally when you allow its expansion through love. In a place of pure gratitude, love is the ultimate choice, an everlasting, impermeable energy.

Trust in the caduceus to hold the love vibration steady in your soul, keeping its channels open to receive its spiritual messages.

Live Fully in the Moment

Spiritual practices promote a dynamic motif: channeling Divine light into your soul. Like an intricate tapestry, your soul has many facets. It yearns for affirmations of Spirit's presence to deepen the relationship.

Nothing transports you to the Divine realm more than the present moment, the now.

Your soul's desire for unity with Spirit necessitates a reconciliation with your past. When you remain stuck in former energetic patterns, you carry regrets throughout your life. Dwelling on unpleasant memories depletes your energy, preventing you from moving forward. Until you disengage from the past, you are unable to manifest your dreams and desires.

Available for your exploration, this is an invitation to discover the power of now.

Present with all your senses, the now brings you into that split second of time, the moment. When you concentrate your attention on the here and now, you give yourself freely. The quality of your focus is clear, neither dwelling on the past, nor worrying about the future.

When you live in the moment, you live your life from a grounded and centered place.

Trusting your instincts to inspire you, you rely on their subtle messages. Calling upon your spiritual guides, allies, and angels, you have complete mastery in a single moment of time to leverage change. It is entirely up to you, using your free will to decide where to plant your focus.

The power of now is indisputable. You have the choice in every moment to step forth and live your life by embracing your blessings and sufferings in one single moment. The ability to change your thoughts, emotions and feelings is at your disposal, a choice that is yours alone.

In dissolution of time and space, your manifestation skills are primed. Interweaving your body, mind and soul into the Divine realm, you become part of the infinite. In this immeasurable energy field, events and circumstances flow in a synchronous manner. It all happens in the moment.

The past and future collapse in this energetic immersion. You discover the beauty and wonder which Spirit brings right here, right now. You are fully present, allowing its light to expand into your field and work its magic.

Your nonphysical intelligence materializes, carrying your Spirit there. Your power is limitless.

Your soul path expands each moment in your life. As your witness, your soul guides you to new avenues of exploration. By aligning with Source, you avoid the urge to find answers to all your questions. Spirit provides interpretations to your queries. In this moment of Divine grace, you accept their implications.

Accessing the power of now, channeling light sanctions your personal relationship with the Divine. Generating the infinite Divine spark within your soul, you reexamine your present reality. Coming to terms with your authentic self, old patterns transform into fresh, hopeful energy. An enlightened space, you and Spirit are one.

Living fully in the moment connects you to the universal wisdom, where you can impact the blueprint of your spiritual Truth.

The Yin-Yang of Life

Existence is about expansion and contraction. Feeling universal energy in our bodies, we apply it to our life circumstances, using it to our advantage. This relationship is central to Divine law. This rhythm is called the yin-yang of life.

Yin-Yang is the concept of duality forming a whole.

Yin and yang elements come in pairs, such as the sun-moon, male-female, light-dark, passive-active, or hot-cold. Seemingly opposite in nature, the yin-yang forces coexist, functioning as a single unit. Because they symbolize life's expansion and contraction, they rely on each other to fuel their individual strengths. Blended, they represent a whole reality, where dualism is merged into one.

The nature of yin-yang lies in the interchange and interplay of the two components. A starting point for change, yin-yang intertwines the many parts of your soul. It highlights your strengths and weaknesses, leaving nothing out.

Resistance, fear, and negative thinking hold you in a contracted, yin state of being. Blocking access to Divine consciousness, you feel closed down and separate from others. Yin energy is an opportunity, a time of introspection.

Expansion occurs at the completion of a yin phase of your life. Moving with ease and grace allows you to receive the lessons, carrying you into a yang period. Yang is a time of openness to the universe, finding gratitude in your growth.

Like the shadow and the light, yin-yang energies complement one another. At completion, your soul is balanced. Yin-yang together bring Divine equilibrium.

The yin-yang of life operates in a symbiotic fashion, ebbing and flowing with the stages of your life.

Be Like the Wind

Be like the wind. Allow it to circulate around and through your body. Invite wind energy into your soul, touching your core with its gentle touch. Like the branches of a weeping willow, wind power is both graceful and dynamic.

Wind provides a cleansing energy, dispelling old or toxic patterns which do not serve your highest good. Unwanted thoughts, feelings and emotions are recycled into the Earth's core, regenerating your vital source. Emulating the wind allows undesirable, toxic experiences to migrate through you.

Horses synchronize our energy with the wind, reminding us to flow with life. Wind is a valuable barometer for us, helping us reset imbalances we feel in our bodies and emotions. Recognizing the disharmonies which diminish our vibrational essence, wind helps us to live with more presence and mindfulness.

We read your wind energy when you approach us. When you resonate with the wind, your light-bearing capability shines through, inviting an authentic partnership. We know when you are honest and live with integrity. Alternatively, we see through the deception, dishonesty and lies. It's simple. We read the energy you emit.

This corresponds with natural law.

Wind is a regenerative force, resetting you from the inside out. Wind power provides you with the ability to discharge anger and frustration building inside your body. Activating your conscious awareness, you feel its effects through practice and repetition. A metaphor for change, wind enables the process of letting go, a step toward spiritual transparency. Wind is your powerful Spirit ally, guiding you to greater equanimity and harmony in your life.

Be like the wind.

Be Like the Wind

Author's Biography

Ellen is a Spiritual Counselor, Energy Healer, Psychic, Medium, Reiki Master Teacher and Animal Communicator.

In her spiritual counseling practice, Ellen performs psychic readings for people and pets. Using clairvoyance, clairaudience, and clairsentience, she reads past lives and the seven layers of the aura, which correspond to the seven chakras. The psychic readings provide valuable information about one's life's journey. Through access to the deepest layers of self, blockages are revealed, thereby increasing self-awareness along the spiritual path.

What follows a spiritual or psychic reading is a new perception of one's life mission, and relationship to the universe.

In Ellen's energy healing sessions, she uses dowsing instruments such as pendulums, dowsing wands and rods to check energy. The energetic checkup ascertains imbalances in the client's physical, emotional, mental, and spiritual needs. Her work can be performed in person, or remotely. The remote healings and readings are quite powerful since they are conducted in a sacred "container" where there are no expectations or interruptions in the energetic exchange.

Using crystals and dowsing techniques for space setting and grounding for all her spiritual practices, Ellen communicates with animals in body and in the Spirit realm. The crystals open up the Divine connection. The dowsing tools offer validation when the thinking mind gets in the way, and validation is necessary. In these silent communication arenas, she hears their messages or sees the images they convey, such as who they are with on the other side.

What follows an animal communication session is closure for those who are grieving a deceased pet, or answers to lingering health or behavioral issues.

One of Ellen's specialties is tracking lost animals. While this can be an emotional and difficult time for clients, sometimes the lost pet will respond to an energetic transmission or communication reassuring him or her that it is safe to go home. In most cases, Ellen can discern a location using dowsing and visualization techniques to find a missing pet.

Tracking lost animals is valuable for pet owners who are distraught and upset when their beloved friend goes missing.

Ellen is also trained in mediumship, conducting readings for people and animals who have crossed the veil to the Spirit Realm. Ellen connects with one's guides and angels during these readings. The information that she transmits is comforting, bringing peace to those on the earthly plane.

Author's Note

Thank you for reading *Be Like the Wind*. My deepest desire is that you found some spiritual nuggets in its contents. If you have a moment, please add your review of the book at your favorite online site for feedback. See my website for information on the upcoming *Be Like the Wind* Tarot deck. Also, if you would like to connect with me, please visit my website:

www.EnlightenedAnimals.com.

6TH
BOOKS

ALL THINGS PARANORMAL

Investigations, explanations and deliberations on the paranormal, supernatural, explainable or unexplainable. 6th Books seeks to give answers while nourishing the soul: whether making use of the scientific model or anecdotal and fun, but always beautifully written.
Titles cover everything within parapsychology: how to, lifestyles, alternative medicine, beliefs, myths and theories.
If you have enjoyed this book, why not tell other readers by posting a review on your preferred book site?

Recent bestsellers from 6th Books are:

The Scars of Eden
Paul Wallis
How do we distinguish between our ancestors' ideas of God and close encounters of an extraterrestrial kind?
Paperback: 978-1-78904-852-0 ebook: 978-1-78904-853-7

The Afterlife Unveiled
What the dead are telling us about their world!
Stafford Betty
What happens after we die? Spirits speaking through mediums know, and they want us to know.
This book unveils their world...
Paperback: 978-1-84694-496-3 ebook: 978-1-84694-926-5

Harvest: The True Story of Alien Abduction
G.L. Davies
G.L. Davies's most-terrifying investigation yet reveals one woman's terrifying ordeal of alien visitation, nightmarish visions and a prophecy of destruction on a scale never before seen in Pembrokeshire's peaceful history.
Paperback: 978-1-78904-385-3 ebook: 978-1-78904-386-0

Wisdom from the Spirit World
Carole J. Obley
What can those in spirit teach us about the enduring bond of love, the immense power of forgiveness, discovering our life's purpose and finding peace in a frantic world?
Paperback: 978-1-78904-302-0 ebook: 978-1-78904-303-7

Spirit Release
Sue Allen
A guide to psychic attack, curses, witchcraft, spirit attachment, possession, soul retrieval, haunting, deliverance, exorcism and more, as taught at the College of Psychic Studies.
Paperback: 978-1-84694-033-0 ebook: 978-1-84694-651-6

Advanced Psychic Development
Becky Walsh
Learn how to practise as a professional, contemporary spiritual medium.
Paperback: 978-1-84694-062-0 ebook: 978-1-78099-941-8

Where After
Mariel Forde Clarke
A journey that will compel readers to view life after death in a completely different way.
Paperback: 978-1-78904-617-5 ebook: 978-1-78904-618-2

Poltergeist! A New Investigation into Destructive Haunting
John Fraser
Is the Poltergeist "syndrome" the only type of paranormal phenomena that can really be proven?
Paperback: 978-1-78904-397-6 ebook: 978-1-78904-398-3

A Little Bigfoot: On the Hunt in Sumatra
Pat Spain
Pat Spain lost a layer of skin, pulled leeches off his nether regions, and was violated by an Orangutan for this book.
Paperback: 978-1-78904-605-2 ebook: 978-1-78904-606-9

Astral Projection Made Easy
and overcoming the fear of death
Stephanie June Sorrell
From the popular Made Easy series, Astral Projection Made Easy helps to eliminate the fear of death through discussion of life beyond the physical body.
Paperback: 978-1-84694-611-0 ebook: 978-1-78099-225-9

Haunted: Horror of Haverfordwest
G.L. Davies
Blissful beginnings for a young couple turn into a nightmare after purchasing their dream home in Wales in 1989.
Paperback: 978-1-78535-843-2 ebook: 978-1-78535-844-9

Readers of ebooks can buy or view any of these bestsellers by clicking on the live link in the title. Most titles are published in paperback and as an ebook. Paperbacks are available in traditional bookshops. Both print and ebook formats are available online.

Find more titles and sign up to our readers' newsletter at
www.6th-books.com

Join the 6th books Facebook group at
6th Books The world of the Paranormal